The Resistance Band Workout Book

The Resistance Band Workout Book

Ed McNeely
and
David Sandler

BURFORD BOOKS

Printed in the United States of America.

10 9 8 7 6 5 4 3 2 1

Library of Congress Cataloging-in-Publication Data

McNeely, Ed (Edward), 1967-
  The Resistance band workout book / Ed McNeely and David Sandler.
      p. cm.
  Includes index.
  ISBN 1-58080-138-2
  1. Bodybuilding. 2. Isometric exercise. I. Sandler, David. II. Title.

GV546.5M394 2006
613.7'13—dc22

2006014947

Contents

CHAPTER 1

The Tubing Advantage

Once reserved solely for rehabilitation settings, rubber tubing has become a staple in fitness and sport performance training. Rubber tubing will allow you to increase muscle strength, power, and speed, helping you to alter your appearance by aiding fat loss and changing the appearance of your muscles.

The benefits of strength training with rubber tubing goes far beyond the performance and appearance changes many people initially seek when they start their training.

Preventing Injuries

Whether you are playing a sport or walking on an icy street, injuries can occur at any time. Stronger bones, muscles, joints, and connective tissue will make you more resistant to the acute injuries that occur during falls or collisions with an opponent, but the real benefits of strength training come in the prevention of the chronic shoulder, knee, and back pains that can make everyday life more difficult.

Muscle imbalances, either bilateral differences between the right and left sides of the body, or agonist/antagonist imbalances in muscles that are on opposite sides of a joint, have been implicated in the development of injury. Muscle imbalances cause the body to move incorrectly, resulting in excessive strain on some muscles and joints. Some studies have noted that a muscle imbalance of greater than ten percent between the right and left sides of the body increase the risk of injury twenty times.

Most sports, and many of our daily activities, force us into a position where one side of the body is used more than the other, leading to muscle imbalances. Tubing is particularly effective at preventing injuries because most of the exercises are unilateral, meaning that the right and left sides work independently, forcing each side to contribute the same amount work to each exercise.

The Anti-Aging Formula

There is a relationship between muscle size and strength. This does not mean that you need to develop huge muscles to become strong—even small increases in muscle size will dramatically increase strength. As we age, there is a decline in muscle mass and strength, leading to chronic aches and pains, difficulty performing daily activities, and a loss of independence and quality of life. This deterioration in performance can start as early as age thirty and gets worse every year, but don't despair; a moderately intense full body strength training program with resistance bands, performed two or three times per week, can delay and even reverse the loss of muscle mass.

It's never too late to start a strength-training program. Muscle mass and strength can increase in people well into their 70s. There are many retired people who are physically stronger and more fit after taking up resistance-band strength training than they were in their youth.

Strength training is a life-long physical activity that also carries with it a variety of health benefits, including improved blood lipid profiles and increased bone density.

ALTERED BLOOD LIPID PROFILES

High blood-cholesterol levels have been associated with the development of heart disease. Controlling cholesterol levels—increasing HDL (the good cholesterol) or decreasing LDL (the bad cholesterol)—can lessen the incidence of heart disease. Strength training has been shown to decrease total cholesterol and improve the LDL/HDL ratio that is strongly linked to health problems by decreasing LDL and increasing HDL levels.

INCREASED BONE DENSITY

Osteoporosis is a widespread problem in modern society, particularly among older people. After age thirty-five, bone density starts to decline at a rate of one to three percent per year. While this may not sound like much, the cumulative effect of years of bone loss can result in bone fractures and overall frailty in old age. We have known for more than a century that there is a relationship between mechanical loading of bone and bone density and strength. Certain types and volumes of physical activity increase bone mineral density (BMD) while immobilization, lack of weight-bearing activity, and prolonged bed rest decrease bone density. Resistance-band strength training, taken up after age thirty-five, is one of the best ways to slow or halt the normal loss of bone density. Taking strength training up earlier in life may provide even more benefits. Strength training during your teens and early twenties can increase bone density, providing you with a buffer against future bone loss. Even if there is a period in your life when you are unable to exercise to maintain your bone density, you have some to spare.

Strength Training for Children

The use of strength training for children has gained acceptance as part of a well-rounded fitness program. The risks of injury to children during strength training are lower than those of most other popular participation sports and the notion that resistance training will damage growth plates in the bones has not been born out by research. A well designed resistance-band strength program that focuses on the individual physical and psychological maturity level of the child can not only decrease the risk of injury in other sports but it can improve bone density, positively alter body composition and increase the child's self esteem. An early, positive strength training experience can foster a lifelong appreciation for physical activity.

Based on the NSCA's position statement and reviews by the American Academy of Pediatrics, the following guidelines are recommended for developing strength training programs for prepubescent children:

➤ Young athletes require a medical examination prior to strength training, including assessing their physical maturity level.

➤ There is no lower limit on age when a child can start strength training. Decisions on starting age should be based more on emotional maturity and the child's ability to follow directions than on physical development.

➤ Provide adequate supervision and instruction. The athlete-coach ratio should not exceed 10:1 with a ratio of 5:1 preferred. This should help the athlete learn proper technique. Most strength training injuries occur because of poor exercise technique.

➤ Prohibit maximal lifts.

➤ Ensure that the athlete is emotionally mature to accept and follow directions. Athletes risk injuring themselves and others when strength training if they cannot follow directions and safety guidelines.

➤ Consider the unique physical and psychological make up of each athlete. Since the rate of emotional and physical maturity varies from person to person an individualized training program will help improve performance and decrease the chance of injury.

➤ Include strength training in a conditioning program. Expose young athletes to a variety of activities and movement patterns. Limiting training to a specific activity can slow the athlete's overall development.

➤ Keep training fun for the athlete. By keeping training fun, the athlete can develop a lifelong appreciation of fitness and sport. The length of the athlete's career can be increased if the level of enjoyment is high.

➤ Develop or adopt a set of weight-training rules and regulations.

Starting children into a strength-training program at an early age may help them develop the skills and attitudes needed to make strength training part of a life long commitment to exercise. Rubber tubing provides an inexpensive initiation to strength training, affording children a safe way to learn the basic body positions and movements before they go on to handle the heavier weights needed in some sports training programs.

Adequate supervision will ensure that the risks of injury often attributed to strength training are minimized, while the benefits, which include increased strength, improved blood lipid profile, enhanced motor skills, and decreased rate of injury in other sports, are maximized in an enjoyable setting.

Safe and Effective Training

Strength training in general is one of the safest forms of physical activity, having a much lower injury rate than other common recreational activities like, basketball, tennis, golf, or running. Training with resistance bands is usually even safer, given the relatively low levels of resistance that are employed. Safe technique is essential, however, in any form of resistance training. As long as some simple guidelines are followed your strength training experience can be injury free.

TECHNIQUE FIRST

Approximately 80% of the injuries that occur during strength training result from poor technique. The purpose of this book is to help you learn how to safely and properly perform a variety of exercises, but ultimately you have responsibility for ensuring that you are doing the exercises properly. If you are not sure how to do an exercise after reading the descriptions it may be worth investing a few dollars to have a personal trainer or strength coach spend an hour showing you the exercises that are causing confusion.

A major cause of technical errors is training to failure. When you push yourself to the point that you can no longer perform the exercise, the last couple of repetitions are usually done with less than perfect technique. During the first four to six months of training, when your body is still learning to perfect the movements, avoid training to failure. Stop the set when you or your training partner first notices that your technique is starting to break down.

NO PAIN MORE GAIN

One of the most persistent myths in strength training is that muscle soreness represents progress and that if you are not sore the next day you did not work hard enough. This is based on the notion that breaking down muscle tissues causes them to increase in size and strength. This attitude oversimplifies a series of very complex physiological changes at the cellular level that involve many hormones, growth factors, and nutrients. There is little scientific evidence that breaking down the muscle is the best stimulus for adaptation. While it is common to be sore for a few days when you take up a training program for the first time, consciously attempting to be sore after every training session will quickly lead to overtraining and a variety of injuries, particularly tendonitis. The tendons do not recover as quickly from the stress of training as the muscles do.

PROGRESSION

It is important to challenge yourself during a training session. The overload principle, one of the primary principles of training, states that the muscles must be put under a continually greater stress if they are to continue to adapt. On the other hand, the need for progress must be tempered with adequate recovery so that your body can adapt to the stress. It is human nature to jump into a new activity with enthusiasm, and while you may have the time to work out six days per week, it does not mean you should. When starting a strength training program begin with two sessions per week, increase to three after three or four months, and then move onto a more advanced program, training four or more times per week after six to eight months of training.

REST

Strength training affects more than the muscles—your bones, connective tissue, heart, and nervous system are all stressed during training. These organs and tissues do not all recover or adapt at the same rate, so while the muscles may have recovered from one training session, connective tissue may still need more time. Since it is not possible to measure recovery in multiple systems, it is essential to plan a recovery week into your training. A recovery week should occur every four to six weeks. This is a week when you decrease the frequency and intensity of your training sessions by cutting the number of exercises, and the resistance you use, in half. This gives all the tissues and organs a break, allowing them to recover and improve at a faster rate.

VARIETY

Your body adapts to an exercise very quickly. One of the reasons that there are many different exercises in this book is to allow you to change the exercises frequently. Varying the exercises will help you progress faster and prevent overuse injuries that may occur when the same exercise is done for too long. Exercises should be changed every three to four weeks.

These guidelines will increase the effectiveness of your program and help keep you injury free, but common sense is always your strongest ally. If something does not feel right during training, don't do it. If you are feeling too tired for a training session, take an extra day off; unless you are training for a major sporting competition an extra day off is not going to affect your progress.

Advantages of Tubing

For many people training with tubing offers all the benefits of strength training with machines and weights, but also enjoys several advantages over these more traditional training methods.

PORTABILITY

The most obvious advantage of using rubber tubing for your strength program is portability. Tubing takes up very little space, and a complete program can be designed using tubing with two or three different resistances along with household items like broom handles, stools, and chairs. This feature makes tubing an ideal training tool for those who want to train at home and have limited space. Tubing can easily fit into an overnight bag or suitcase when you are traveling, allowing busy professionals to get in their workouts on the road.

COST

Tubing is one of the most cost effective strengthening tools available, starting at under $5 for a single tube. A complete home tubing gym can be developed for under $75. The low price makes tubing the ideal equipment for settings like physical education and group fitness classes.

FREEDOM OF MOTION

Tubing offers nearly complete freedom of motion. It can be adjusted to any size and shape of body and can be used in an unlimited number of positions. The freedom of motion that is inherent in tubing means that you can exercise not only the major muscles but also the smaller, stabilizing muscles whose strength is important for preventing injury.

Tubing can simulate sports movements more closely than what can be obtained using free weights or machines. One of the main principles in sport-conditioning training is called "transfer of training." Transfer of training refers to the amount of sport performance improvement that comes from a certain exercise or training method. For example, if you increased the amount you can bench press by 100%, and your basketball free throw improves by only one percent, you have a 1% transfer of training. It is impossible to simulate a sport activity completely with any type of resistance training, but the closer you can come to the actual movement the greater the rate of transfer. In some instances the tubing can actually be attached to the sport implement to ensure a closer simulation.

Many strength-training machines lock you into a pattern of fixed movements that are dictated by the pulley, cam and track arrangement of the machine. This restriction makes them very effective for training the primary muscles, but much less effective at working the stabilizer muscles. The latest pulley devices from companies like Free Motion and Life Fitness come close to replicating the variety and freedom of motion that you get from tubing, but even they are limited to a certain number of preset positions.

SPEED AND POWER

Speed of movement is an important factor in developing sport-specific strength and power. Sport movements like swinging a golf club or a tennis racquet, hitting a baseball, and kicking a soccer ball are all done at high speed with relatively low resistance. Low-tension tubing allows you not only to use the rotational movement patterns needed to excel at these sports, but also to perform the movements at close to game speed, further increasing the transfer of training.

STRENGTH AT THE END OF THE RANGE OF MOTION

In a normal free-weight exercise, you are limited to the amount of weight you can lift at the weakest point in the exercise. For instance if you are doing a full squat you will find the weak point occurs when your knees are bent at about 140 degrees, and you are much stronger as you get closer to the top of the movement. When you are restricted to using a weight that you can lift at the bottom of the exercise, you are getting little training effect in the top part of the movement. Tubing and other elastic-resistance devices increase their resistance as they are stretched; adding elastic resistance to a free weight bar, in addition to the weights, allows you to increase strength throughout the whole range of motion by loading the muscle at the end of the range of motion where it is strongest. This type of training has become popular with strength and power athletes.

Limitations of Tubing

While tubing is a valuable tool for developing strength and muscular fitness, it does have limitations.

RESISTANCE

Even though there are a variety of tensions of rubber tubing, very strong people and athletes in strength and power sports often require greater resistances than can be developed using tubing alone. As noted above, many competitive athletes attach tubing or large elastic bands to the weights they are lifting to add more resistance at the top of multijoint movements like squats or bench presses.

PROGRESSION

It is difficult to quantify your performance when using tubing. There are no resistance numbers when you are using tubing, so you do not know how much "weight" you are lifting. You know you are increasing resistance if you are using a thicker tube, but you must buy your tubing from the same manufacturer. Unfortunately there are no standards among different manufacturers for tubing tension or resistance, so a half-inch tube from one company may have more or less tension than a half-inch tube from a different company.

Despite these few limitations tubing is an economical, portable training tool that will help you meet your strength, power and fitness goals.

CHAPTER 2

Getting Started

The Basics

The popularity of strength training has increased immensely over the past 25 years, moving from a fringe activity practiced only by bodybuilders and competitive lifters to become a mainstream activity that is recognized not only for its performance-enhancing benefits but also for its ability to improve health and quality of life.

Before you begin your tubing strength program or start reading through the exercise descriptions contained in this book it is essential that you are familiar with some basic concepts in strength training.

Muscle Actions

A muscle action refers to the state of activity of a muscle. Muscles are capable of three types of activity:

➤ *Concentric* muscle actions involve the shortening of the muscle and usually occur when the body or a weight is lifted.

➤ *Eccentric* muscle actions involve lengthening of a muscle and usually occur when a weight is being lowered or the body is decelerated. Landing from a jump involves an eccentric contraction of the quadriceps muscles.

➤ *Isometric* muscle actions involve no change in the length of a muscle. The maintenance of body positions during strength training exercises is accomplished through isometric muscle actions.

ANATOMY

In order to design your training program and fully understand which exercises to choose you need a basic understanding of the anatomy of the major muscles. The figures below highlight the major muscles of the front and back of the body.

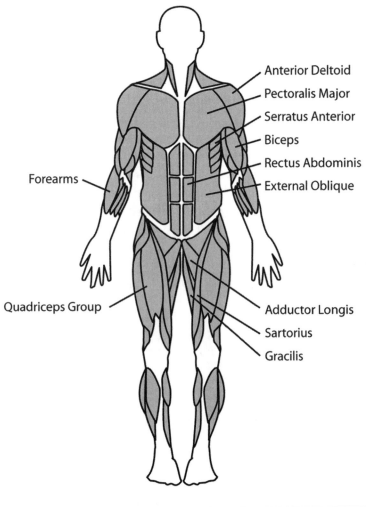

Anterior Deltoid

Pectoralis Major

Serratus Anterior

Biceps

Rectus Abdominis

External Oblique

Forearms

Quadriceps Group

Adductor Longis

Sartorius

Gracilis

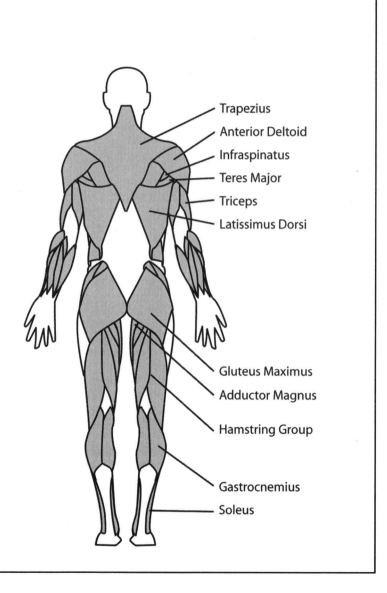

Trapezius
Anterior Deltoid
Infraspinatus
Teres Major
Triceps
Latissimus Dorsi

Gluteus Maximus
Adductor Magnus

Hamstring Group

Gastrocnemius
Soleus

Training Variables
SETS AND REPETITIONS

In strength training a movement cycle consists of a concentric and an eccentric contraction. This cycle is known as a repetition or "rep." When several repetitions are performed in a row this is known as a "set." The number of sets and repetitions that are performed during a training session depends upon the age and experience of the athlete as well as the goals of the training session. This information is covered in more detail throughout the rest of this book.

INTENSITY

Intensity is the amount of tension or stress put on the muscle. Intensity is influenced by the number of sets and reps, and the amount of rest between sets, but mostly intensity is affected by the resistance of the tubing or the amount of weight that is being lifted. Intensity is relative: what is intense for one person may be quite easy for another.

VOLUME

Volume is defined as the total amount of work. It is most often determined by multiplying the sets and reps for each exercise to get a total number of repetitions per exercise. In some cases this is multiplied by the amount of weight lifted for each exercise to get a total amount of weight lifted in the workout.

REST

Rest refers to the amount of time that is taken between sets or exercises. For instance if you do a set of bench presses, and then wait three minutes before you do another set, your rest period was three minutes.

RECOVERY

Recovery refers to the period of time between training sessions that work the same muscle group or exercise. If you did a bench press as part of your workout on Monday, and then did it again on Wednesday, you would have had two days or 48 hours recovery.

Body Planes and Motion

Knowing how the body moves in an important first step when taking up strength training. There are three planes of movement that correspond to the three dimensions of space and four major types of movement.

SAGITTAL PLANE

The sagittal plane is a vertical plane, passing from front to back, dividing the body into right and left halves.

FRONTAL PLANE

The frontal plane is a vertical plane dissecting the body from one side to the other, dividing it into front (anterior) and back (posterior) halves.

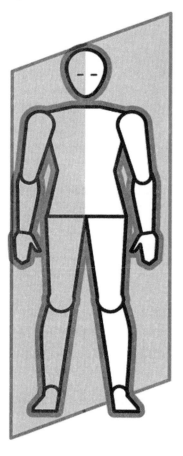

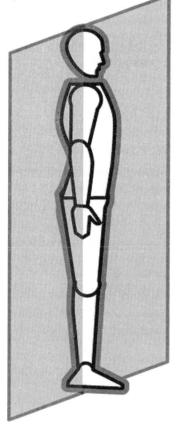

TRANSVERSE PLANE

The transverse plane is a horizontal plane dividing the body into upper and lower halves.

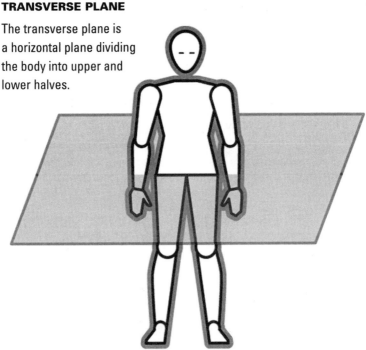

FLEXION

Flexion is a movement in which the angle at a joint diminishes. For instance, there is flexion of the elbow occurring in the arm curl exercise.

EXTENSION

Extension is the opposite of flexion—the angle at the joint increases.

ABDUCTION

Abduction occurs when a limb is moved away from the midline of the body. This term is most often used in sideward movements of the upper limbs away from the body, as in the lateral raise.

ADDUCTION

Adduction occurs when a limb moves towards the midline of the body. This is the opposite of abduction.

GRIPPING THE TUBE

Gripping the tube is an often-overlooked component of strength training. A firm grip on the tube is essential for safe performance of the exercises. A good grip will improve your ability to contract the muscles of the upper body that stabilize you during lifting. There are three different hand grips that can be employed.

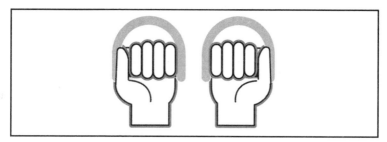

UNDERHAND GRIP

The underhand grip is used mainly for arm curl exercises. The palms are facing forward and the thumbs are wrapped around the handle of the tubing.

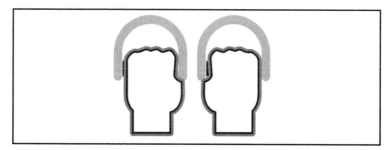

OVERHAND GRIP

This is the most common grip, the palms are placed over the handle and are facing away from the body. This grip is used in pressing movements, squats, pulldowns, various rows and many tricep exercises.

NEUTRAL GRIP

The neutral grip is the most common grip if you are using bands or tubing that does not have a handle. The tubing is held in the palm of the hand with the palms facing medially.

THUMBLESS OR OPEN GRIP

If you read fitness magazines you will undoubtedly see someone using a thumbless grip, where the bar is placed on the heel of the hand and the fingers but not the thumb are wrapped around the bar. This is the least secure of the grips, providing the least control; this grip should never be used with tubing. A thumbless grip increases the chance that the tubing will slip out of your hand, potentially snapping you and causing bruises or welts.

Selecting Your Tubing

There is a wide variety of tubing available from different manufacturers. Tubing is generally colored; unfortunately the resistance that corresponds to the colors from one manufacturer may not be the same for another, making it difficult to choose tubing based on color alone. Most companies carry three to five different tensions, ranging from very light to very heavy. Since tubing is relatively inexpensive, having one tube of each tension level will ensure you have an adequate resistance for a variety of exercises. Double tubing—two pieces of tubing attached to the same handle—is available for stronger people.

Tubing can be purchased either as bulk tubing or in pre-cut lengths. Bulk tubing can be purchased in rolls of up to 100 feet, allowing you to cut different lengths and set up multiple stations. Pre-cut tubing typically comes in 36-, 48- or 60-inch lengths. Most pre-cut tubing has handles, making it much easier to perform most exercises. We recommend the pre-cut tubing with handles for home and personal use and bulk tubing if you are buying for a large group or team.

Some tubing comes with a protective sleeve that protects the tubing from nicks, cuts, sweat, body oils, exposure to UV light and other factors that will cause the rubber to degrade. The sleeve also makes it more comfortable to perform exercises in which the tubing may be rubbing over your body. Whether you choose tubing with a sleeve or not is completely a personal choice; there is no performance advantage to having the sleeve.

SPECIALTY TUBING

The basic tubing with a handle will be adequate for most people. However, there are some specialty tubing and elastic-resistance products that will benefit specific groups of people. "O" tubing is a circular tubing unit that attaches around the ankles and is used to target the inner and outer thighs. This is popular for those who are doing group fitness classes or following fitness videos.

Lateral steppers or resistors are tubing products that feature ankle cuffs joined by a piece of tubing; these are used to add resistance to various agility drills, particularly lateral movement drills. If you are involved in a sport that requires change of direction, speed and agility you may want to consider this product.

Bands, large elastic bands that are draped over a weightlifting bar, have become popular in powerlifting and strength-sports circles. Bands are used in addition to weights to increase the resistance at the top of many multi-joint movements. Powerlifting coach Louie Simmons popularized the use of bands and has had great success using them with top-level powerlifters. There are a variety of sizes of bands, the strongest of which will add up to 150 lbs of resistance to each side of the bar per band attached.

Sprinting resistors and assistors are long pieces of thick tubing that attach to a belt that is worn around the waist. The tubing is held by a training partner and can be used to provide resistance to forward, backward and lateral sprinting exercises. This type of training helps improve stride rate, one of the key components of running faster.

Tubing Accessories

You can get a great workout from tubing alone, but there are a few accessories that you may want to consider if you are making tubing your sole form of resistance training. These accessories increase the number of exercises that you can do, providing more variety to your program.

Wall rails are pieces of wood with hooks every two inches that are attached vertically to a wall. The hooks provide a variety of heights for attaching your tubing, so that you can perform overhead pulling and standing press movements. An alternative to the wall rail is an assist strap that attaches to the tubing and a doorknob, doorjamb or other fixed object.

A tubing platform is a 3' x 3' piece of plywood fastened to a frame made of 2"x 4" boards. Hooks are screwed into the frame every two to three inches. The platform allows you to do various jumps with tubing and makes it easier to do overhead presses, squats and various deadlift movements.

An adjustable bench that lies flat and has various degrees of incline will make it easier to do many of the lying and seated exercises. These benches can be purchased at most big-box department stores for a reasonable price.

Adjusting the Resistance of Your Tubing

As tubing is stretched the resistance increases; the longer the tubing is stretched, the harder it gets to stretch it further. For many exercises you will stand on the middle of the tubing with one foot so that there is equal resistance in each hand. Adjusting your foot position will increase or decrease the resistance. Standing on the tubing with both feet will increase the resistance, and moving your feet apart will increase it even further. If you stand nearer one end of the tubing you will increase the resistance at the end closest to your foot and decrease the resistance at the other end. If you attach your tubing to a wall rail or doorjamb, standing further away from the attachment will increase your resistance.

It is very important to keep track of where you stand in relation to attachment points and where you put your feet on the tubing. This will help you monitor your improvement and make sure that your workouts are consistently done with the same or greater resistance.

Caring for Your Tubing

Modern exercise tubing has come a long way from the surgical tubing that was used years ago. There is a wider range of resistances available, stretchability is greater and the tubing lasts longer. While tubing is very safe, it is not indestructible, and over time it will wear out or break. To get most use from your tubing there are some simple maintenance steps you can follow:

INSPECT YOUR TUBING BEFORE EACH USE

Nicks and cuts will decrease the strength of the tubing and lead to break-age. If you notice a cut in your tubing it is time for a replacement. Do not store you tubing in a box with sharp objects or tools and keep it away from sharp corners if you are tying it to benches or attaching it to door frames. If your tubing has handles inspect the grommets where the tubing is attached to the handle, as this is the point most likely to break.

STORE IN A WARM PLACE

Tubing can become brittle if stored in the cold. Avoid using tubing when it is cold; if it is cold, allow it to warm up for twenty to thirty minutes before it is stretched. Storing tubing in the cold will decrease the life of the tub-ing. If you live in an area that experiences cold temperatures in winter you should keep your tubing in the house, not the garage or the trunk of your car.

WIPE IT DOWN

Always wipe your tubing down with a clean, wet cloth after a training ses-sion. The salts and oils on your skin and in your sweat can dry the tubing, making it brittle. A wet cloth will remove the salts and extend the life of your tubing. Some cleaners and disinfectants can weaken rubber so read the label carefully before using it on your tubing, and if you are not sure, stick with water.

CHAPTER 3

Chest and Arm Exercises

The arms are the simplest body part to train using tubing. Virtually any exercise you can do with a dumbbell or barbell can be duplicated with tubing, without adding any accessories or other equipment. Performing many of the chest exercises will require a chair or a weightlifting or picnic-table bench.

BENCH PRESS Wrap a piece of tubing under a weightlifting or picnic- table bench. Lie down on your back on the bench and grasp one end of the tubing in each hand. Starting with your hands beside your chest, press the tubing to arm's length. Lower the tubing back to chest level. Keep your feet planted firmly on the floor to help you maintain your balance. If your feet cannot reach the floor place a phone book or small stool under each foot to give yourself a firm base of support.

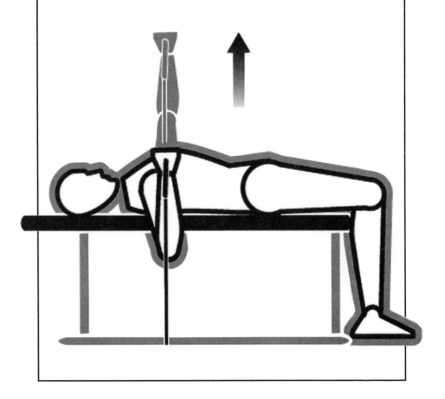

RESISTED PUSH UP Wrap a piece of tubing around your shoulders and upper back, holding it at chest level. You may need to use a shorter piece of tubing or adjust your handhold so that the tubing is taught but not tight around your shoulders. Assume a push up position on the floor with one end of the tubing under each hand. Push yourself up, keeping your body straight and back flat. Lower yourself back to the ground. The tubing will add resistance making the push up harder than normal; if you cannot do a regular push up you should not attempt the resisted push up. Some people may find the tubing digs into their back, making it uncomfortable to do the exercise. If this is the case wrapping a towel around the tubing can provide some padding.

CROSSOVERS Stand between two pieces of tubing attached above shoulder height; feet shoulder width apart. Grasp the handles with an overhand grip. Incline your trunk to about 30 degrees and with elbows slightly bent pull the handles together in front of your body. The movement used in the crossover is similar to hugging a tree, with your hands following a semi-circular path.

ONE ARM FLYS Lie on your back on a weightlifting or picnic table bench. The tubing should be attached to the bench or to a floor level hook or placed under a door. Keeping your arm bent to about 15 degrees reach to the side and grasp the tubing handle in an underhand grip, palm facing the ceiling. Pull the tubing from floor height across your body, keeping your elbow slightly bent. Slowly lower your arm back towards the floor along the same arc.

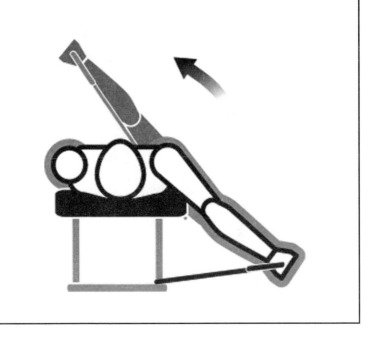

SEATED BENCH PRESS Sit in a high backed chair and wrap the tubing around the chair at chest height. Grasp the handles with an overhand grip and press them to arm's length. Return the handles towards the chest, stopping just before your chest. Keep your feet flat on the floor and head and shoulders against the chair throughout the movement.

INCLINE BENCH PRESS Sit on an incline weightlifting bench or a high backed chair that reclines. The chair or bench should be inclined to about 45 degrees. Wrap the tubing around the bench and grasp the tubing using an overhand grip. Starting with the hands at shoulder height, press the tubing upwards and backwards to that your upper arms are at the side of your head when your arms are straight. Lower the handles back to shoulder height. Try to keep your feet firmly planted on the floor and if you are using a chair be careful that you do not push with your legs and knock the chair over backwards.

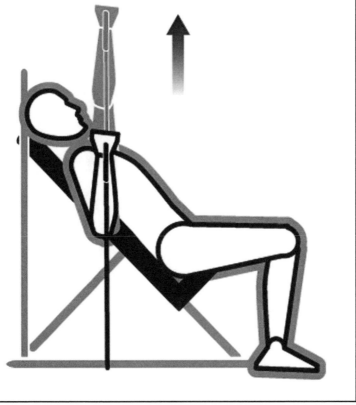

ARM CURLS   Stand with feet shoulder width apart, one foot slightly ahead of the other. Stand on the middle of the tubing with the front foot and grasp the handles with an underhand grip. Starting with your hands at hip height flex both of your upper arms and curl the handles towards your shoulders.
Do not swing your upper body to help the movement. You can increase the difficulty of the exercise by keeping your feet side by side and standing on the tubing with both feet, increasing the distance between your feet to increase the tension on the tube.

ALTERNATE ARM CURLS Stand with feet shoulder width apart, one foot slightly ahead of the other. Stand on the middle of the tubing with the front foot and grasp the handles with an underhand grip. Starting with your hands at hip height flex one of your upper arms and curl the handle towards your shoulder.

As you lower the handle start to curl the other handle. Try to establish a rhythm of raising one handle as you lower the other. Do not swing your upper body to help the movement. You can increase the difficulty of the exercise by keeping your feet side by side and standing on the tubing with both feet, increasing the distance between your feet to increase the tension on the tube.

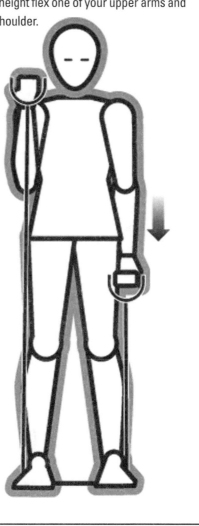

OVERHEAD ARM CURLS Attach the tubing to an overhead hook on a wall rail or wedge it into the top of a doorjamb. Kneel, facing the wall rail, with the handle of the tubing above your head at arm's length. Grasp the handle of the tubing in one hand with an underhand grip. Flex your elbow and curl the handle towards your forehead. Straighten your arm and repeat for the number of reps required before switching arms. Do not bend from the waist or lean back to make the exercise easier.

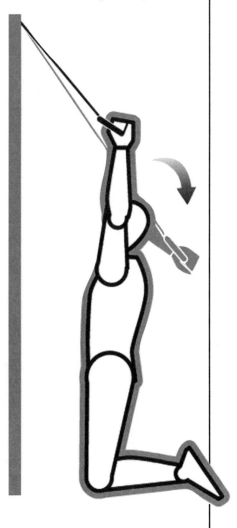

CONCENTRATION CURLS Sit on the end of a flat bench, feet spread apart. Bend over slightly and place your left elbow against the inside of your left knee. Place the left foot on your tubing so that there is six to eight inches of tubing and the handle between your feet. Grasp the handle with an underhand grip and, using your knee to support your arm, curl the handle up as high as you can without lifting your elbow off your knee. Slowly lower the handle until your arm is straight. When you have completed the required repetitions switch arms and stand on the tubing with your right foot.

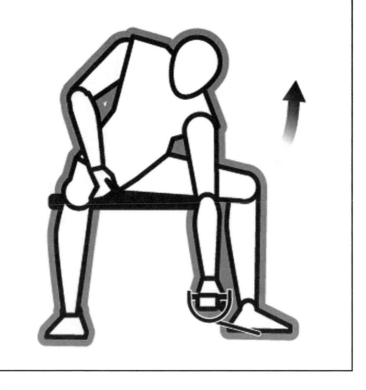

OVERHEAD TRICEPS EXTENSION Stand upright with feet shoulder width apart, knees slightly bent. Stand on one end of the tubing with the heel of one foot. Pull the tubing up behind your body so that the handle is directly behind your head and neck high. Keeping your upper arms perpendicular to the floor, bend your elbows and grasp the tubing in both hands with a palms-in grip. Keeping your elbows pointed towards the ceiling, straighten your arms towards the ceiling. Your upper arms should stay still throughout the movement. Standing further up the tubing will increase the difficulty of the movement.

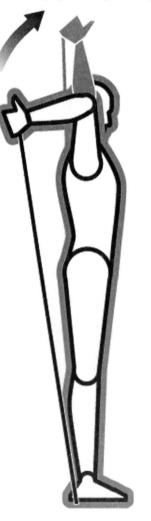

LYING TRICEPS EXTENSIONS Tie a length of tubing around the leg of a weightlifting or picnic table bench. Lie flat on the bench, feet flat on the floor, hold the tubing in both hands with an overhand grip, your arms extended over your chest. Keeping your upper arms perpendicular to the floor, bend your elbows and lower the handle of the tubing until it is just above your face. Keeping your elbows pointed towards the ceiling, extend your arms until they are straight. Your upper arms should stay still throughout the movement.

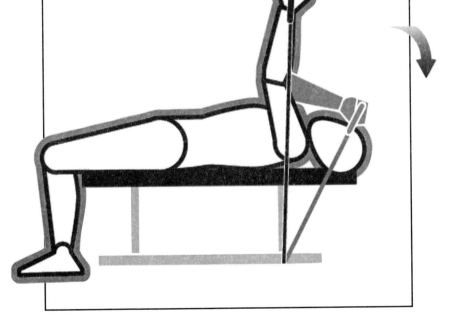

TRICEPS PUSHDOWN Attach the tubing to a high hook on the wall rail or place it over the top of a door. Grasp the handle with a neutral, palms-in grip, hands just outside your hips, arms straight and the handle at waist height. Keeping your elbows tucked into your sides and upper arms still, bend your elbows, bringing your hands up as high as possible while still keeping your elbows tight against your sides. Push the handle back down, following the same arc used during the lift.

SINGLE ARM TRICEPS PUSHDOWN Attach the tubing to a high hook on the wall rail or place it over the top of a door. With one hand grasp the handle in an underhand grip, hand just outside your hip, arm straight and the handle at waist height. Keeping your elbow tucked into your side and upper arm still, bend your elbow, bringing your hand up as high as possible while continuing to keep your elbow tight against your side. Push the handle back down following the same arc used during the lift.

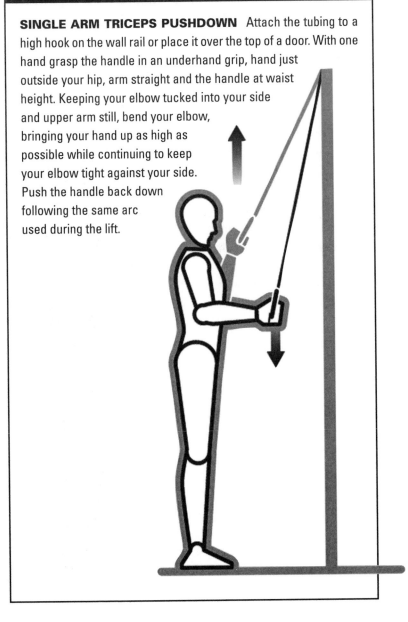

ONE ARM OVERHEAD TRICEPS EXTENSION Stand upright with feet shoulder width apart, knees slightly bent. Stand on one end of the tubing with the heel of one foot. Pull the tubing up behind your body so that the handle is directly behind your head; neck high. Keeping your upper arm perpendicular to the floor, bend your elbow and grasp the tubing in one hand with a palms up, overhand grip. Keeping your elbow pointed towards the ceiling, straighten your arm. Your upper arm should stay still throughout the movement.

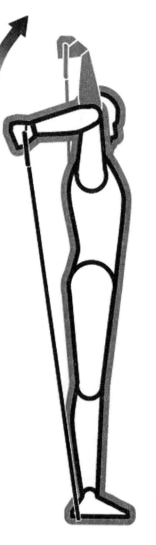

CHAPTER 4

Shoulder Exercises

UPRIGHT ROW   Stand in the middle of a single piece of tubing with two handles, with your feet shoulder width apart. Grasp one handle in each hand with an overhand grip; hands six to eight inches apart. Keeping your upper body still, pull the handles up until they are level with the top of your sternum. Pause and lower them back to the starting position. Be sure to keep your elbows above your hands at all times.

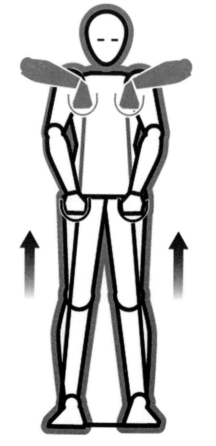

SHRUGS Stand in the middle of a single piece of tubing with two handles, with your feet shoulder width apart. Grasp one handle in each hand with an overhand grip; hands to the sides of your body, palms facing your legs; feet shoulder width apart, knees slightly bent. Slowly shrug your shoulders, raising them as high as possible. Pause for a moment at the top and lower them slowly, back to the starting position.

BENT LATERAL RAISES Stand in the middle of a single piece of tubing with two handles. Cross the handles and grasp the tubing with palms facing each other. Sit on the end of a bench and bend at the waist so that your chest is on your thighs and the tubing handles are just behind your calves. Keeping your elbows slightly bent raise your arms to the side until they reach shoulder level and are parallel to the floor. Pause at the top of the movement and slowly lower your arms. Try to create a straight line across the shoulders from hand to hand; do not let the hands drift backwards as you raise your arms.

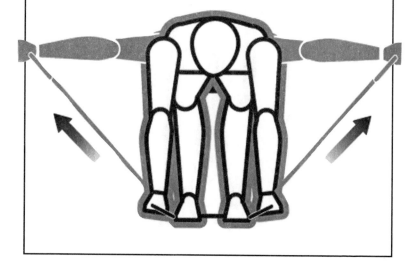

SIDE LATERAL RAISES Hold a piece of tubing in each hand, standing on one end, or stand in the middle of a piece of tubing with two handles so that the handles are at waist height. Grasp the handles with palms facing each other. Keeping the elbows slightly bent raise your arms directly to the side until they reach shoulder level and are parallel to the floor. Pause at the top of the movement and slowly lower your arms. Do not swing your body to help you lift the weight.

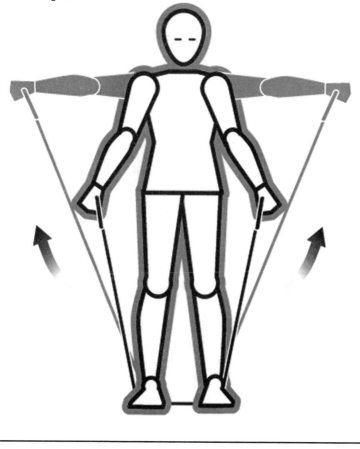

FRONT RAISES Standing up straight, hold a piece of tubing in each hand, standing on one end, or stand in the middle of a piece of tubing with two handles so that the handles are at waist height. Keeping the elbows slightly bent, raise your arms directly in front of you until they reach shoulder level and are parallel to the floor. Pause at the top of the movement and slowly lower your arms. Do not swing your body to help you lift the weight.

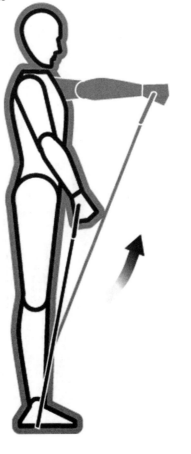

REAR RAISE Standing up straight, stand on a piece of tubing so that the handle is to the side of your leg at arm's length. Grasp the handle with your palm facing forward. Keeping your elbow slightly bent, raise your arm directly backwards as high as you can without bending forward. Pause at the top of the movement and slowly lower your arm. Do not swing your body to help you lift the weight.

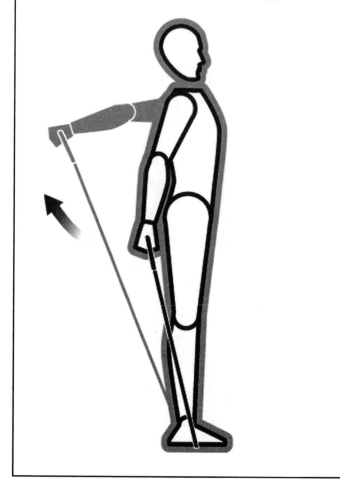

45° RAISE Standing up straight, stand on a piece of tubing so that the handle is halfway between the side and front of your leg and at waist height. Grasp the tubing so that your thumb is pointing towards your leg. (It may be easier to hold the tubing rather than the handle for this exercise.) Keeping your elbow slightly bent, raise the tubing straight up from your thigh until your arm is at shoulder level and is parallel to the floor. Pause at the top of the movement and slowly return to the starting position. Do not swing your body to help you lift the weight.

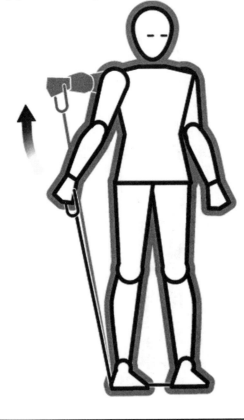

EXTERNAL ROTATION   Attach a piece of rubber tubing to a doorknob or other apparatus so that it is just above waist height. Grasp the tubing in one hand so that it stretches across your body and has some tension. Bend your elbow to 90 degrees. Keeping you elbow close to your side, rotate your arm outwards, away from your body as far as possible.

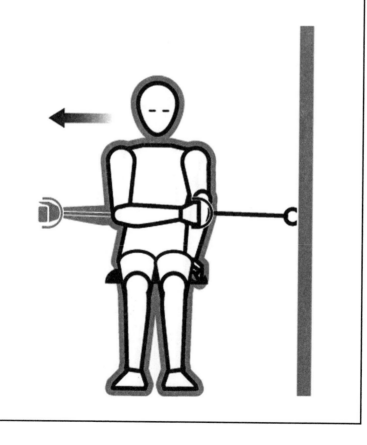

INTERNAL ROTATION Attach a piece of rubber tubing to a doorknob or other apparatus so that it is just above waist height. Bend your elbow to 90 degrees and rotate your arm so that your forearm is perpendicular to your body. Grasp the tubing in one hand so that it has some tension. Keeping your elbow close to your side, rotate your arm inwards, towards your body as far as possible.

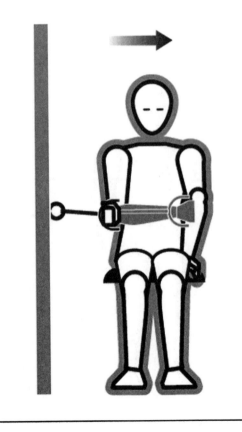

OVERHEAD INTERNAL ROTATION Stand with feet shoulder width apart, tubing attached to a shoulder high hook, and grasp the tubing with an overhand grip, palm facing forward. If you do not have a wall rail you can attach the tubing to a doorknob and kneel rather than stand. Raise your arm so that your upper arm is parallel to the floor. Bend your elbow to 90 degrees so that your forearm is perpendicular to your upper arm with the palm of your hand facing forward. Keeping your upper arm parallel to the floor, rotate from your shoulder so that the handle of the tubing moves downwards towards the floor. Following the same arc used to lower, pull the weight back up to the starting position.

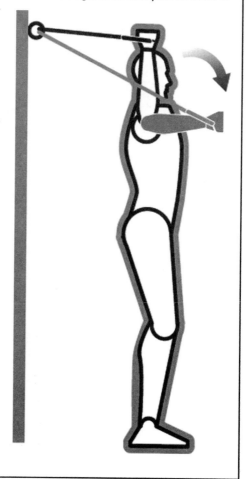

OVERHEAD EXTERNAL ROTATION Stand with feet shoulder width apart, tubing attached to a shoulder high hook, and grasp the tubing with an overhand grip, palm facing forward. If you do not have a wall rail you can attach the tubing to a doorknob and kneel, rather than stand. Raise your arm directly to the side so that your upper arm is parallel to the floor. Bend your elbow to 90 degrees so that your forearm is perpendicular to your upper arm with the palm of your hand facing the floor. Keeping your upper arm parallel to the floor, rotate from your shoulder so that the handle of the tubing moves backwards over your head. Following the same arc, lower the handle back to the starting position.

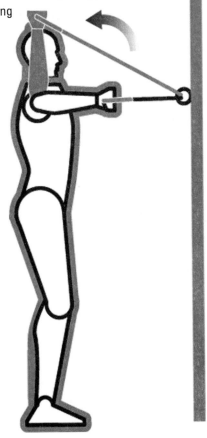

90-90 INTERNAL ROTATION Stand with feet shoulder width apart, tubing attached to a shoulder high hook, and grasp the tubing with an overhand grip, palm facing forward and the tubing perpendicular to your arm. If you do not have a wall rail you can attach the tubing to a doorknob and kneel, rather than stand. Raise your arm straight in front of you so that your upper arm is parallel to the floor. Bend your elbow to 90 degrees with the palm of your hand facing the midline of your body. Keeping your upper arm parallel to the floor rotate from your shoulder so that the handle of the tubing moves downwards towards the floor. Following the same arc raise your forearm back until it is perpendicular to the floor.

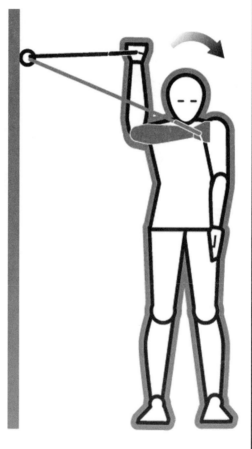

90-90 EXTERNAL ROTATION Stand with feet shoulder width apart, tubing attached to a shoulder high hook, and grasp the tubing with an overhand grip, palm facing forward and the tubing perpendicular to your arm. If you do not have a wall rail you can attach the tubing to a doorknob and kneel, rather than stand. Raise your arm straight in front of you so that your upper arm is parallel to the floor. Bend your elbow to 90 degrees so that your forearm is perpendicular to your upper arm with the palm of your hand facing the floor. Keeping your upper arm parallel to the floor rotate from your shoulder so that your forearm moves until it is perpendicular to the floor. Following the same arc lower tubing back up to the starting position.

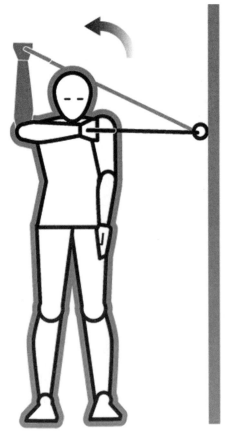

OVERHEAD PRESS Hold a piece of tubing in each hand, standing on one end, or stand in the middle of a piece of tubing with two handles so that the handles are at waist height. Grasping the handles in an overhand grip bring them to shoulder height so that your palms face away from your body. Keep your head up, chest out, and shoulders back. Your back should be flat with a slight arch at the base; feet are shoulder width apart. Press the handles overhead until your arms are fully extended. Bend the elbows and control the handles back down to the shoulders and the starting position.

SEATED OVERHEAD PRESS Hold a piece of tubing in each hand, standing on one end, or stand in the middle of a piece of tubing with two handles so that the handles are at waist height. Sit on the end of a bench or in a straight back solid chair. Grasping the handles in an overhand grip bring them to shoulder height so that your palms face away from your body. Keep your head up, chest out, and shoulders back. Your back should be flat with a slight arch at the base. Press the handles overhead until your arms are fully extended. Bend the elbows and control the handles back down to the shoulders and the starting position.

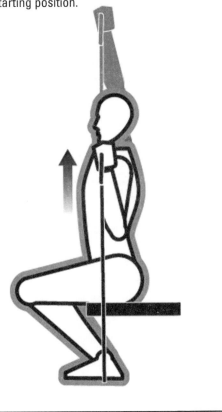

ALTERNATING OVERHEAD PRESS Hold a piece of tubing in each hand, standing on one end, or stand in the middle of a piece of tubing with two handles so that the handles are at waist height. Grasping the handles in an overhand grip bring them to shoulder height so that your palms face away from your body. Keep your head up, chest out, and shoulders back. Your back should be flat with a slight arch at the base; feet are shoulder width apart. Press one handle overhead until your arm is fully extended. As you lower the handle start to press the other overhead. Try to establish a rhythm of pressing one handle up while lowering the other.

ALTERNATING SEATED OVERHEAD PRESS Hold a piece of tubing in each hand, standing on one end, or stand in the middle of a piece of tubing with two handles so that the handles are at waist height. Sit on the end of a bench or in a straight back solid chair. Grasping the handles in an overhand grip, bring them to shoulder height so that your palms face away from your body. Keep your head up, chest out, and shoulders back. Your back should be flat with a slight arch at the base. Press one handle overhead until your arm is fully extended. As you lower the handle start to press the other overhead. Try to establish a rhythm of pressing one handle up while lowering the other.

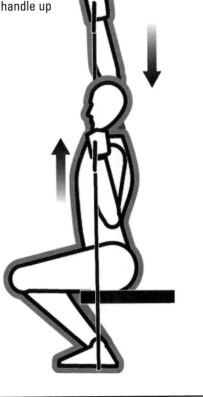

LOW TRAP EXERCISE Stand in the middle of a single piece of tubing with two handles. Grasp the tubing with an overhand grip, thumbs facing each other. Sit on the end of a bench and bend at the waist so that your chest is on your thighs and the tubing handles are just behind your calves. Keeping your trunk on your thighs, head neutral and thumbs facing each other, raise the tubing until your arms are beside your ears. Pause for one second and slowly lower the handles.

THUMBS UP LOW TRAP EXERCISE Stand in the middle of a single piece of tubing with two handles. Grasp the tubing with palms facing each other, thumbs pointed towards the ceiling. Sit on the end of a bench and bend at the waist so that your chest is on your thighs and the tubing handles are just behind your calves. Keeping your trunk on your thighs, head neutral and thumbs up, raise the tubing until your arms are beside your ears. Pause for one second and slowly lower the handles.

THUMBS DOWN LOW TRAP EXERCISE Stand in the middle of a single piece of tubing with two handles. Grasp the tubing with backs of the hands facing each other, thumbs pointed towards the floor. Sit on the end of a bench and bend at the waist so that your chest is on your thighs and the tubing handles are just behind your calves. Keeping your trunk on your thighs, head neutral and thumbs down, raise the tubing until your arms are beside your ears. Pause for one second and slowly lower the handles.

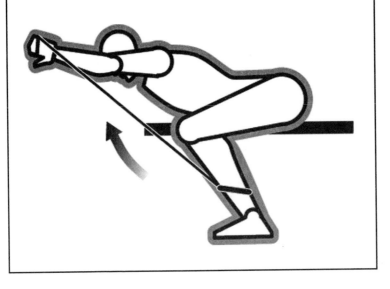

CHAPTER 5

Leg and Hip Exercises

HIP EXTENSION Attach the tubing to an ankle-high hook or under a door. Facing the door, place your foot through the handle or wrap the tubing around your ankle. Stand upright, feet shoulder width apart, and hold onto a broomstick or some other support. The leg that is working should be extended in front of your body ten to twelve inches. Keeping the torso upright, move the leg with the tubing straight backwards as far as possible, pause, and return slowly to the starting position. Do not bend forward from the waist to try to increase the range of motion;
maintain an upright torso at all times.

HIP FLEXION Attach the tubing to an ankle-high hook or under a door. Facing away from the door, place your foot through the handle or wrap the tubing around your ankle. Stand upright, feet shoulder width apart, and hold onto the machine or some other support. The leg that is working should be extended behind your body ten to twelve inches. Keeping the torso upright, bend the leg with the tubing and raise your knee straight forwards as far and as high as possible, pause, and return slowly to the starting position. Do not bend forward from the waist to try to increase the range of motion; maintain an upright torso at all times.

HIP ADDUCTION Attach the tubing to an ankle-high hook or under a door. Facing sideways, place your foot through the handle or wrap the tubing around your ankle. Stand upright, feet shoulder width apart and hold onto a pole or some other support. The leg that is working should be extended in to the side of your body 18-24 inches. Keeping the torso upright, move the leg with the tubing across your body as far as possible, pause, and return slowly to the starting position. Do not bend forward from the waist to try to increase the range of motion; maintain an upright torso at all times.

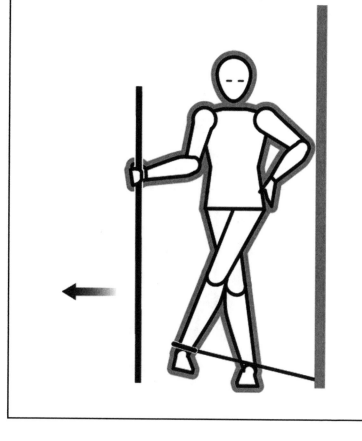

HIP ABDUCTION Attach the tubing to an ankle high hook or under a door. Facing sideways, place your foot through the handle or wrap the tubing around your ankle farthest from the door. Stand upright, feet shoulder width apart and hold onto a pole or some other support. The leg that is working should be crossed in front of your body six to eight inches. Keeping the torso upright, move the leg with the tubing straight sideways as far as possible, pause, and return slowly to the starting position. Do not bend forward from the waist to try to increase the range of motion;
maintain an upright torso at all times.

HIP INTERNAL ROTATION Attach the tubing to an ankle high hook or under a door. Sit on the floor with legs straight in front of you, ten to twelve inches apart, facing sideways to the door. Place the handle of the tubing over the top of the foot closest to the door so that the handle is at the ball of your foot, or wrap the tubing around your toes. Sitting up straight, rotate your foot inwards towards the floor. Return to the starting position and repeat for the required number of repetitions.

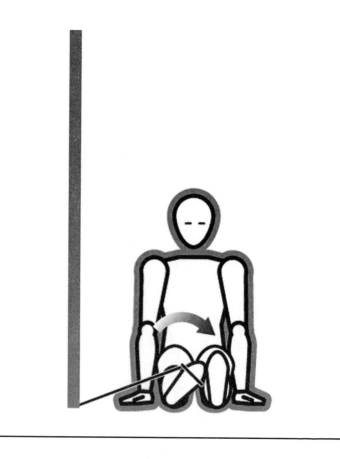

HIP EXTERNAL ROTATION Attach the tubing to an ankle high hook or under a door. Sit on the floor with legs straight in front of you, ten to twelve inches apart, facing sideways to the door. Place the handle of the tubing over the top of the foot furthest from the door so that the handle is at the ball of your foot, or wrap the tubing around your toes. Sitting up straight, rotate your foot outwards, away from your body. Return to the starting position and repeat for the required number of repetitions.

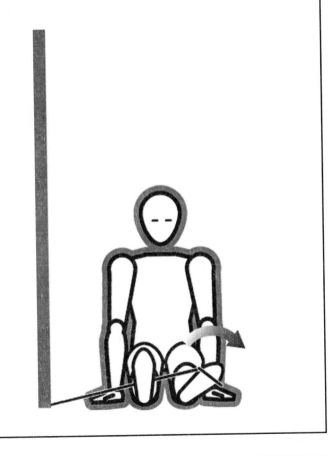

SQUAT Stand with feet shoulder width apart on a piece of tubing with two handles. Slip a broomstick through the handles of the tubing and raise the bar over your head, onto your back, just above your posterior deltoids. One strand of tubing should be on each side of your body. Place your hands just outside your shoulders on top of the handles to prevent them from slipping during the movement. Keep your head up, chest out, and shoulders back. Your back should be flat with a slight arch at the base; feet are shoulder width apart.

Point your toes outwards at an angle of 30-35°. Inhale deeply and contract the muscles of the torso to help stabilize your upper body and keep your back flat. Descend by slowly lowering the buttocks towards the floor, keeping your hips under the bar as much as possible. Descend until the tops of the thighs are parallel to the floor. The ascent starts with a powerful drive to accelerate yourself out of the bottom position. Keep your head looking up to help counter forward lean. Keep the muscles of your torso contracted throughout the ascent phase of the lift. Continue to push with your legs until you come to a full standing position. Take another deep breath and descend for the next rep.

SPLIT SQUATS Stand with both feet in the middle of a short piece of tubing holding a handle in each hand. Raise your hands to shoulder height. Keeping your torso upright take a long step backward with one leg, allowing the front leg to bend to 90°. The back leg should be slightly bent. Keeping your torso upright at all times, push off the heel of the front foot and straighten the front leg, then lower yourself back to the starting position. Do not step back to the upright position until you have done the required number of repetitions, then stand upright and switch legs, repeating the same number of repetitions.

SINGLE LEG SEATED LEG PRESS Sit in a straight back chair and straighten one leg so that it is parallel to the floor. Place the handle of the tubing over your foot so that the ball of your foot is against the handle and your toes point towards the ceiling. Hold the tubing tightly in your hands. Bend your knee so that your thigh moves towards your body. Straighten your leg, pressing the tubing handle away from you. Pause for a second and allow your knee to bend towards your body again. Straighten but do not lock your leg during this movement.

STANDING LEG CURL The standing leg curl is done one leg at a time. Attach the tubing under a door or on an ankle-high hook. Slip your foot through the handle or wrap the tubing around your ankle. Step away from the door so that there is some tension on the tubing. Holding onto a broomstick or some other support to help you maintain your balance, curl your leg and raise your heel towards your buttocks. When you have reached the top position, pause and slowly lower your foot back to the start. Do all repetitions with one leg before switching to the other.

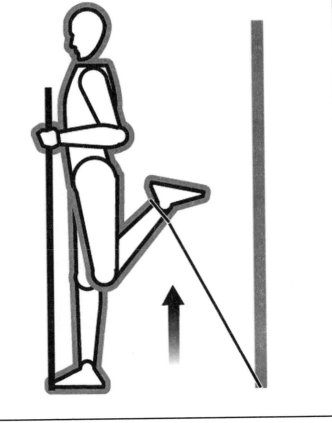

SINGLE LEG LYING LEG CURL Lie face down on a bench with your knees just off the end of the bench. The tubing is attached under a door, to the leg of the bench or on a low wall rail hook. Slip your foot through the handle of the tubing so that the handle is across your Achilles tendon or wrap the tubing around your ankle. Hands should be holding onto the bench. Keeping your upper body flat against the bench, curl your legs and raise your heel towards your buttocks. When the full range of movement has been completed lower your foot back to the starting position. Try to keep your hips on the bench at all times.

THE CLAM Lie flat on your side, supporting your head with your arm, legs together and knees bent to 45 degrees. Slip an O tube around both legs at knee height. Keeping your feet together rotate from the hip, opening your knees like a clam shell opening. Bring your knees back together and repeat as required.

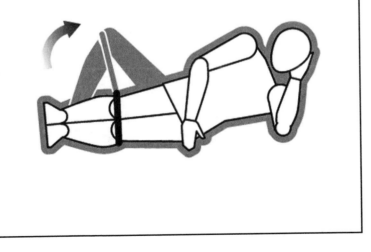

O-TUBE ABDUCTION   Lie flat on your side, supporting your head with your arm, legs together and bent to 10 degrees. Slip an O tube around both legs at ankle height. Raise the top leg straight up as high as possible. Lower the leg back down and repeat for the required number of repetitions before rolling over to work the other leg.

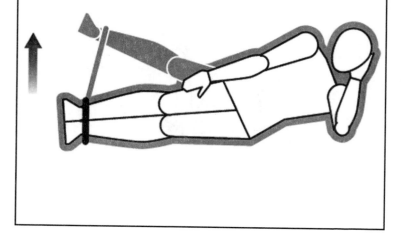

GLUTE PRESS Kneel on all fours, holding one end of the tubing under one hand. Slip the foot on the same side through the handle of the tubing so that the handle is at the ball of your foot. Press your leg straight back so that your leg is just above parallel to the floor. Bring your knee as close to your chest as possible and press it out again. This is an excellent exercise to work your buttocks.

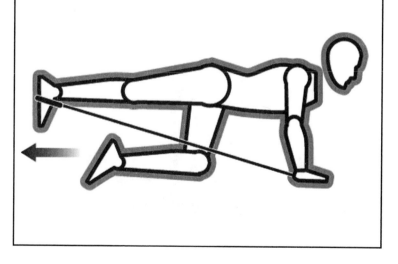

SEATED CALF RAISE The seated calf raise works the soleus muscle, the muscle that lies under and below the gastrocnemius, the larger calf muscle. Sit on a chair of bench with the balls of your feet on a phone book or small block of wood. Cross the handles and stand on the tubing near the handles so that it can be looped over your knee. Bend at the ankles, lowering your heels towards the floor. Rise up on your toes as high as possible, pausing at the top for a second before lowering to the fully stretched position again.

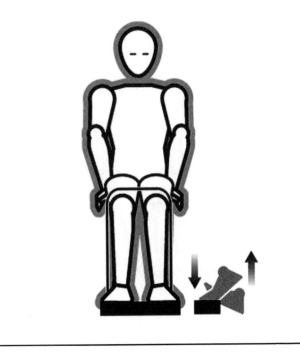

STANDING CALF RAISE Stand with the balls of your feet on a block four to five inches high, feet shoulder width apart, tubing under your feet. Slip a broomstick through the handles of the tubing and raise the bar over your head, onto your back, just above your posterior deltoids. One strand of tubing should be on each side of your body. Lower your heels towards the floor as low as possible while keeping the balls of your feet on the block. Lift yourself by rising up on your toes as high as possible, pausing at the top for a second before lowering to the fully stretched position. Keep your legs straight but not locked throughout the movement to make sure the movement is coming from the ankle and that you are not lifting yourself with the other leg muscles.

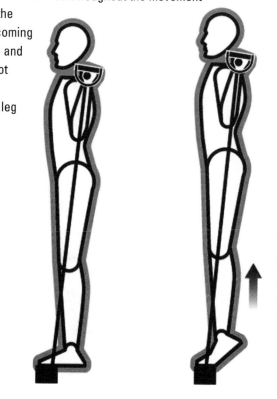

SEATED CALF PRESS Sit in a straight back chair and straighten one leg so that it is parallel to the floor. Place the handle of the tubing over your foot so that the ball of your foot is against the handle and your toes point towards the ceiling. Hold the tubing tightly in your hands. Straighten your ankle, pressing the tubing handle away from you. Pause for a second and allow your ankle to bend backwards as far as possible. Keep your legs straight but not locked throughout the movement to make sure the movement is coming from the ankle and not the other leg muscles.

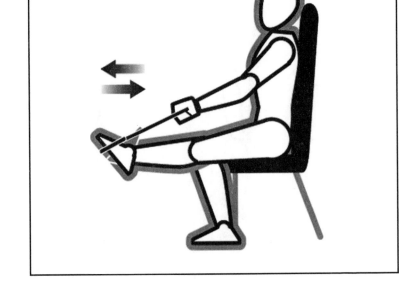

CHAPTER 6

Back Exercises

STANDING ROW Wrap the tubing around a waist high hook or immovable object. Grasp the tubing with an overhand grip and take two steps away from the hook so that there is tension on the tubing. Bend your knees slightly and, keeping your head up and back straight, brace your body by contracting your abdominal muscles and pull the handles in until they touch your stomach.

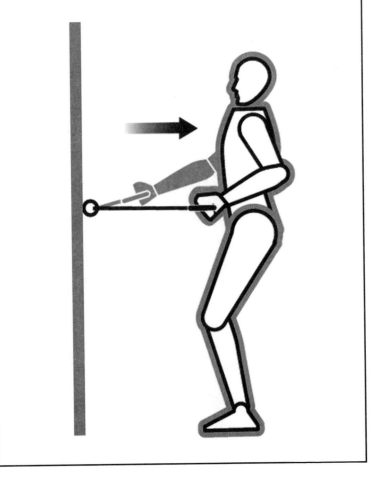

STRAIGHT ARM PULLDOWN Attach the tubing to a high wall rail hook or loop it over the end of a door so that the handle is just above your head. Stand or kneel in front of the tubing, an arm's length away from the door or wall, arms extended overhead. Take a handle in each hand with an overhand grip with hands slightly wider than shoulder width apart. Keeping your arms straight, pull both handles straight down in front of your body until they come to hip level. Do not swing your body or sit back to help with the movement.

ALTERNATE-ARM STRAIGHT ARM PULLDOWNS Attach the tubing to a high wall rail hook or loop it over the end of a door so that the handle is just above your head. Stand or kneel in front of the tubing, an arm's length away from the door or wall, arms extended overhead. Take a handle in each hand with an overhand grip with hands slightly wider than shoulder width apart. Keeping your arms straight, pull one handle straight down in front of your body until the handle comes to hip level. As you let the handle return to the starting position overhead pull the other handle straight down to hip height. Do not swing your body or sit back to help with the movement.

THE DEADLIFT Slip a broomstick through the handles of your tubing. Stand on the tubing, with feet shoulder width apart and the broomstick close to your shins. Squat down and grasp the bar with a mixed grip (one hand underhand, the other overhand). Your feet are flat on the floor, hips are low, back is flat, head is up and shoulders are over the broomstick. Initiate the movement by pressing your legs into the floor, lifting the weight. Keeping the weight close to your body continue to lift with your legs until the broomstick passes your knee caps then bring your hips through and stand up straight. Incline your trunk forward slightly and bend your knees to lower the broomstick straight down to the floor. Keep your hips low, chest out and shoulders back throughout the movement to keep your back flat and injury free.

STRAIGHT LEG DEADLIFT Slip a broomstick through the handles of your tubing. Stand on the tubing, with feet hip width apart and the broomstick close to your shins. Bend at the waist, keeping the legs almost straight, with about 10 degrees of knee bend. Grasp the broomstick with an overhand grip, placing the hands slightly wider than shoulder width apart. Your head is up, chest is out, and shoulders are back. Your back is flat with a slight arch at the base. Keeping the broomstick as close to your body as possible, slowly pull the weight up keeping your arms fully extended and your back flat. Think about keeping your trunk muscles tight and squeeze your buttocks as your straighten up. Slowly lower the broomstick back to the floor following the opposite path you used during the lift, reset your body and repeat for the required number of repetitions.

PULLDOWNS Attach the tubing to a high wall rail hook. Kneel on the floor and take an overhand grip with hands slightly wider than shoulder width apart. Incline your trunk backwards about 10 degrees and pull the handles down in front of the body until they touch the top of the sternum. Slowly return the handles to the starting position. Keep the body still throughout the movement.

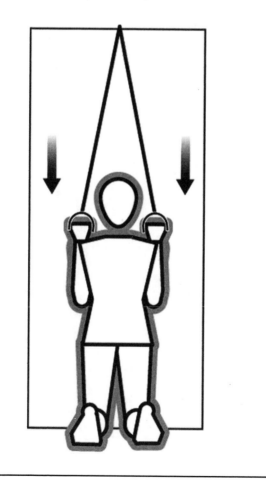

ALTERNATE PULLDOWNS Attach the tubing to a high wall rail hook or loop it over the end of a door. Kneel in front of the tubing and take a handle in each hand with an overhand grip with hands slightly wider than shoulder width apart. Incline your trunk backwards about 10 degrees and pull one handle down in front of the body until it touches the top of the sternum. Slowly return the handle to the starting position and pull the other handle down. Keep the body still throughout the movement and try to establish a rhythm of pulling one handle down while letting the other return to the starting position.

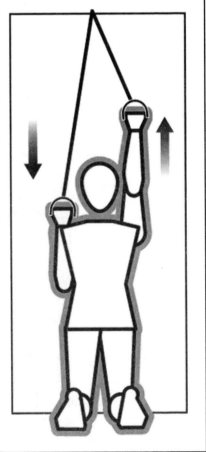

ONE ARM PULLDOWNS Attach the tubing to a high wall rail hook or loop it over the top of a door. Kneel in front of the tubing and take a handle in one hand with an overhand grip with hands slightly wider than shoulder width apart. Incline your trunk backwards about 10 degrees and pull one handle down in front of the body until it touches the top of the sternum. Slowly return the handle to the starting position and pull the other handle down. Keep the body still throughout the movement.

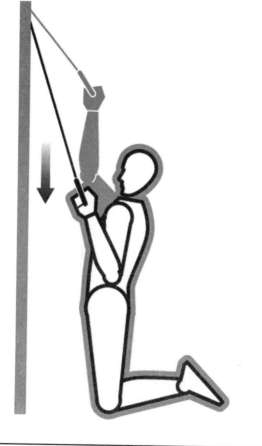

SEATED ROW Sit on the floor with legs straight in front of you. Loop the tubing around your feet and sitting upright, grasp the handles with a narrow overhand grip. Your legs are straight and your back is flat. Bending forward from the hips about 20 degrees, pull the handles towards your body initially by straightening the back. Once the handle reaches your knees use the arm to finish the pull and bring the handle to the base of your sternum.

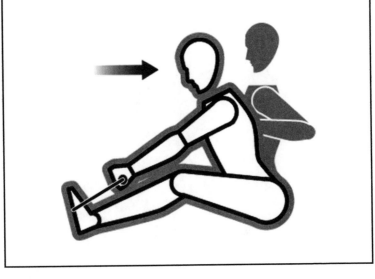

ONE ARM SEATED ROW Sit on the floor with legs straight in front of you. Loop the tubing around your feet and sitting upright, grasp one handle with a narrow overhand grip. Your legs are straight and your back is flat. Bending forward from the hips about 20 degrees pull the handle towards your body initially by straightening the back. Once the handle reaches your knees use the arm to finish the pull and bring the handle to the base of your sternum.

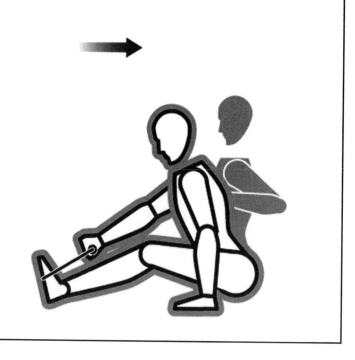

CHAPTER 7

Trunk and Abdominal Exercises

SIDE BENDS Hook one end of the tubing under a door. Stand so that the tubing is beside one leg; bend to the side as far as possible and grasp the tubing at arm's length. Bend to the other side as far as possible, dragging the tubing up your leg. Slowly bend back to the starting position. Your trunk should be bending from side to side only, do not bend forward or backward.

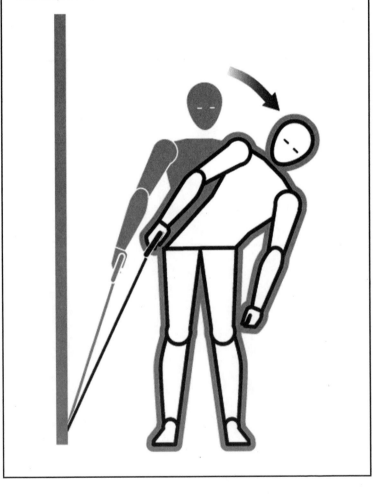

WOOD CHOPS Attach the tubing to a high wall rail hook or over the top of a door. Stand directly in front of the tubing and reach up to grasp the handle with both hands. Keeping the arms straight, pull the tubing down in front of you, bending from the waist as if you were chopping a piece of wood with an axe.

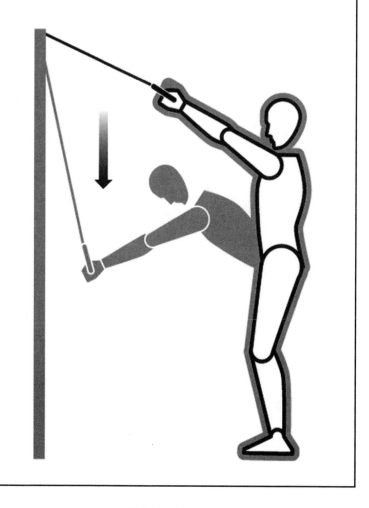

CURL UPS Slide the tubing under a door. Lie flat on your back perpendicular to the door, knees bent so that your feet are flat on the floor, the tubing by your head. Reach back and grasp the tubing with both hands so that the handle of the tubing is near your forehead and your elbows point towards the ceiling. Curl your trunk up until your shoulder blades are fully off the floor. Slowly uncurl until you are flat on your back again and repeat as required.

OVERHEAD CRUNCHES Attach the tubing to a high wall rail hook or over the top of a door. Kneel directly in front of the tubing, facing away from the door; reach up to grasp the handle with both hands. Pull the tubing handle down until your hands are even with the top of your head. Using your abdominal muscles, curl yourself down until your elbows touch your knees. Slowly return to the upright position and repeat as required. Be sure to keep your arms still throughout the movement so that they do not contribute to the motion.

TRUNK ROTATIONS Attach the tubing to a waist high hook or loop it around a doorknob. Stand facing parallel to the door and grasp the handle of the tubing with both hands. Rotate your trunk so that your hands point towards the doorknob and step away from the door so that the tubing is taught. Keeping your arms straight, rotate your trunk as far as possible in the opposite direction. After completing the required number of repetitions face the opposite direction and repeat.

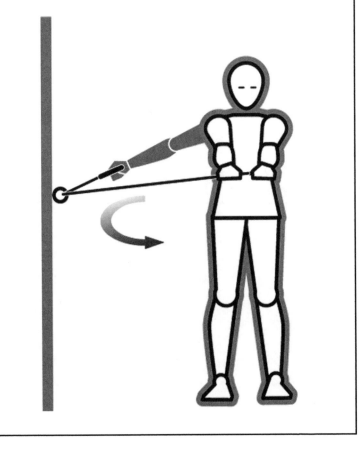

PADDLERS Attach the tubing to a high wall rail hook or over the top of a door. Kneel on one knee directly in front of the tubing, facing the door; reach up to grasp the handle with both hands. Pull the tubing down and to the side so your hands finish beside the knee that is on the ground. The motion should be similar to that used in paddling a canoe or Dragon boat. When you have completed the desired number of repetitions switch legs and repeat on the other side.

TWISTING OVERHEAD CRUNCHES Attach the tubing to a high wall rail hook or over the top of a door. Kneel directly in front of the tubing, facing away from the door; reach up to grasp the handle with both hands. Pull the tubing handle down until your hands are even with the top of your head. Using your abdominal muscles curl yourself down until your right elbow touches your left knee. Slowly return to the upright position and on the next repetition the left elbow will touch your right knee. Continue alternating like this until you have completed the desired number of repetitions. Be sure to keep your arms still throughout the movement so that they do not contribute to the motion.

LEG TUCKS Attach the tubing to a low hook or slide it under a door. With legs straight, hold the tubing between your feet or tie it around your ankles. Sit on the end of an exercise bench or on the edge of a hard backed chair so that your buttocks are just on the edge of the bench. Your hands are just behind you hips; incline your trunk back at a 45 degree angle. Keeping your trunk inclined pull your knees towards your chest. Straighten your legs and repeat as required.

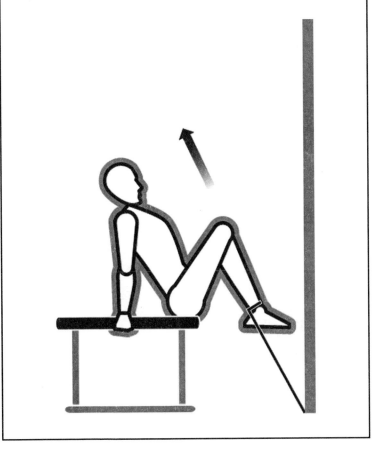

LEG RAISES The leg raise is the next progression from the leg tuck and should only be done after several weeks of doing leg tucks. Attach the tubing to a low hook or slide it under a door. With legs straight hold the tubing between your feet or tie it around your ankles. Sit on the end of an exercise bench or on the edge of a hard backed chair so that your buttocks are just on the edge of the bench. Your hands are just behind you hips; incline your trunk back at a 45 degree angle. Keeping your trunk inclined and legs straight raise your legs as high as possible. You should be able to raise them high enough that your legs and trunk form a V.

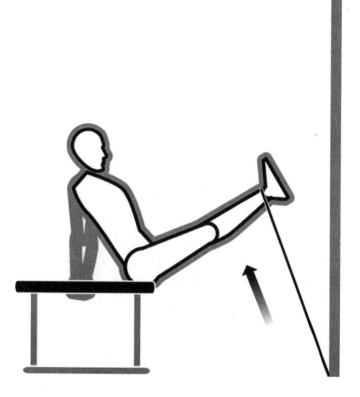

STABILITY BALL SIDE BENDS Hook one end of the tubing under a door. Sit on a stability ball so that the tubing is beside one leg; bend to the side as far as possible and grasp the tubing at arm's length. Bend to the other side as far as possible, dragging the tubing up your leg. Slowly bend back to the starting position. Your trunk should be bending from side to side only, do not bend forward or backward. You can increase the difficulty of the exercise by lifting one leg off the floor.

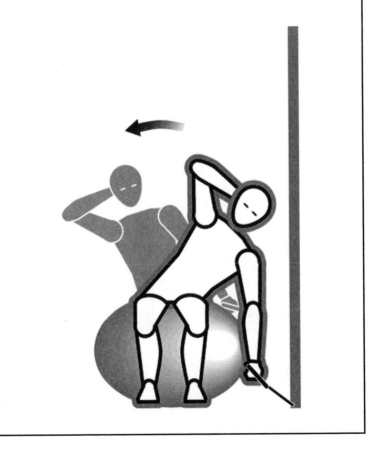

STABILITY BALL WOOD CHOPS Attach the tubing to a high wall rail hook or over the top of a door. Sit on a stability ball directly in front of the tubing and reach up to grasp the handle with both hands. Keeping the arms straight, pull the tubing down in front of you, bending from the waist as if you were chopping a piece of wood with an axe. You can increase the difficulty of the exercise by lifting one foot off the ground.

STABILITY BALL TRUNK ROTATIONS Attach the tubing to a waist high hook or loop it around a doorknob. Sit on a stability ball facing parallel to the door and grasp the handle of the tubing with both hands. Rotate your trunk so that your hands point towards the doorknob and step away from the door so that the tubing is taught. Keeping your arms straight, rotate your trunk as far as possible in the opposite direction. After completing the required number of repetitions face the opposite direction and repeat. You can increase the difficulty of the exercise by lifting one foot off the ground.

CHAPTER 8

Sport Specific Exercises

S port specific exercises simulate part or all of a sport skill. The objective of these exercises is to build sport specific strength, speed and power. Sport specific exercises will normally only be used after developing a good overall strength base using general exercises. Because they simulate all or part of your sport movement, these exercises can have a positive impact on your performance. There are several principles detailed below that must be followed to use these exercises effectively.

Use a light tube

Sport movements are done at high speed with little resistance. If you use a piece of tubing that provides too much resistance you will struggle to perform the exercises using the same technique that you would in your sport. This may alter the way you perform in the game, decreasing your performance. The light tube also allows you to work at close to game speed with a little more resistance, increasing speed and power. If the resistance is too great you will increase strength at a lower speed, which will not help your play.

Resistance Early

You will need to adjust the tubing so that there is resistance early in the range of motion. Most of the power for sport events is developed in the first part of the movement and is finished with the momentum you generate. To train this pattern you need to have the tube stretched so that there is adequate resistance at the start of the movement. You may even want to consider only performing the first half of many movements, since the final half of most throws, kicks, and ball-striking movements is done purely with momentum.

Work Antagonists

Antagonist muscles are those that oppose a movement. For instance when throwing a baseball the muscles on the front of the body initiate the movement and give it power. The muscles on the backside of the body, like the rotator cuff, stop the movement and help prevent injury. If the antagonist muscles are not strong enough, you will develop chronic injuries. Use some of the general exercises outlined in the other chapters to make sure that you have a balanced program.

It would be impossible to list all of the sport specific tubing exercises in this chapter and we do not claim to be experts in the technique of all sports, so what we have done is include several classifications of exercises that will benefit most from tubing work. We will explain the general set up and who will benefit from the exercise, but we are leaving it up to you to ensure that the technique that you employ is as close as possible to your sport technique.

Punches

Boxers and martial artists use tubing punch techniques. Jabs, crosses and uppercuts are all easily performed.

JABS For a jab attach the tubing at shoulder height and step forward so that there is tension on the tube. Assume the position you would use when throwing a jab for your sport, holding the tubing in the hand that will be jabbing. To more closely simulate most jab techniques the tubing should be just outside your jab arm. Using the appropriate footwork and body action, throw a jab. Control the movement back and throw another. Focus on the speed of the movement.

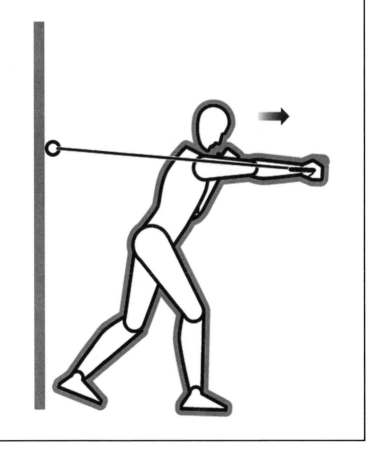

CROSSES When performing a cross the tubing will need to be attached at shoulder height to the side of your body. Since the hand arcs outwards during a cross you will need to step far enough away from the anchor point so that there is still tension on the tube as it arcs away from the body before crossing back to the target point. Again be sure to use proper footwork and body motion.

UPPERCUTS Uppercuts require the tubing to be attached at floor height. If you do not intend to step into the uppercut you can stand on the tubing. Make sure to stand low enough on the tubing so that tension is on the hand at the start of the punch. Use proper body and arm mechanics and throw the uppercut as fast as possible.

With all the punches it is important to control the tubing on the way back so that you do not get into the habit of letting your arm fall back to the starting position. Some coaches believe in actively returning the punch arm to its starting position. If you ascribe to this belief you can work the return portion of the punches by attaching the tubing directly opposite to what you would use to throw the punch and pull the arm back to the start position against the tubing resistance.

BACKHANDS Racquet sport athletes such as tennis, squash and racquetball players will use tubing backhands. They are less appropriate for badminton players who use a lot more wrist action. Attach the tubing to a shin high hook or object. Stand with the hook to one side of your body and the tubing stretched across your body. Step away from the anchor point so that there is tension on the tube and position your body as if you were hitting a backhand. Allowing your arm to stretch across your body use proper footwork and body motion to swing the tubing through your backhand motion. To make the movement more sport specific you can tie one end of the tubing to a racquet handle similar to the one you play with. The tubing should be attached just above your hand; attaching it higher up or on the head of the racquet will change your swing too much.

FOREHANDS Racquet sport athletes such as tennis, squash and racquetball players will use tubing forehands. They are less appropriate for badminton players who use a lot more wrist action. Attach the tubing to a shin high hook or object. Stand with the hook to one side of your body the tubing on the same side. Step away from the anchor point so that there is tension on the tube and position your body as if you were hitting a forehand. Allowing your arm to stretch away from your body, use proper footwork and body motion to swing the tubing through your forehand motion. To make the movement more sport specific you can tie one end of the tubing to a racquet handle similar to the one you play with. The tubing should be attached just above your hand; attaching it higher up or on the head of the racquet will change your swing too much.

KICKS A variety of athletes will use kick exercises while training for their sport; soccer players, football kickers, and martial artists to name a few. Wrap the tubing around your ankle and attach it to a low hook. Position your body as if you were about to perform a kick for your sport; for football and soccer players you should start standing upright with feet hip width apart. Step forward and swing your leg as if you were kicking a ball. Make sure to follow through. The tubing should be tight enough to provide resistance but not so tight that it pulls you off balance as you perform the kick.

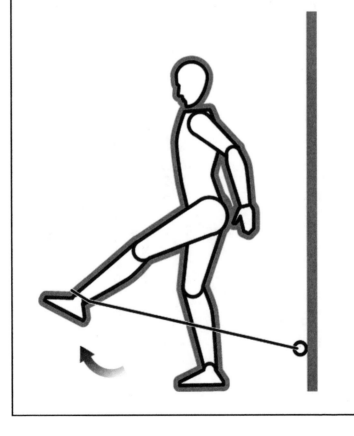

SHOT PUTS Shot putters who do not have an indoor facility that allows them to throw either shots or medicine balls in the off season can use tubing to work on the final rotation and arm action. Attach the tubing to a low anchor and stretch it so that there is tension on the tube. Stand on one leg and bend forward as if you were in the last part of your glide, just as you enter the turn. Using good shot-put technique, turn and drive the arm through as if your were throwing; stretch the tube through to your finish position.

SWINGS Golfers and baseball players use swings to develop hip rotational power for striking the ball. Attach one end of the tubing to a belt loop at the side of your body on the back leg when in your swinging stance. The other end of the tubing is attached to a waist high anchor directly in back of you. Step away from the anchor so that there is tension on the tube and assume your stance. Using your normal bat or club swing at an imaginary ball or hit a practice ball. Focus on firing the back hip through the movement, working against the tubing resistance. Some people will practice swings by attaching the tubing to the golf club or baseball bat. This is less effective than the method described here because it does not allow the resistance to be attached where the power is developed.

THROWS A variety of athletes will use throws while training for their sport; football quarterbacks, volleyball players and baseball players will benefit from throw simulations. Attach the tubing to an overhead anchor at hand height when your hand is coming through the highest point of your throw. Stand in your starting throw position, wind up and step forward into your throw, making sure to maintain proper throw mechanics and arm positioning. There should be tension on the tube when your arm is extended behind your body during the wind up.

WIND UPS Wind ups are the opposite of throws, working the movement where the ball or racket is taken away from the body. Attach the tubing to a waist high anchor and grasp the other end with one hand, using a grip similar to that used in your sport. Position your body as you would when winding up to throw a ball or swing your racquet. Move your arm through your normal wind up motion against the resistance provided by the tubing, pause at the top and return to the start.

CHAPTER 9

Speed and Power Exercises

Tubing is an excellent tool for developing speed and power. Power is the optimal combination of speed and strength and in many sports the speed component is more important than the strength component. Tubing exercises allow you to effectively perform movements at high speed with little risk of injury.

Running speed is a key performance factor for many sports. The ability to run quickly in a straight line is only part of the equation; change of direction, lateral and backwards running all need to be developed if an athlete is to truly excel. Improving running speed is a combination of technical work, to improve body position and running mechanics, and physical training. Tubing allows you to perform resisted runs, which will increase running strength and assisted runs, which will help improve leg turnover rate, one of the key ingredients in running fast.

The drills presented here should be incorporated into an overall sport conditioning program based on the demands of your sport and your starting level.

SPRINT WITH PARTNER RESISTANCE Two people with comparable speed are paired up for this drill. One wears the belt with the sprint resistor tubing attached, the other holds the loose end tightly. The tubing should be taut, with little slack. It is important to keep constant tension on the tubes but not overstretch them. Begin with one partner lined up in front of the other. The partner in front starts to run, when they have gone about 5 yards the other partner starts to follow at a slightly slower pace so that the tubing continues to stretch and the resistance increases. As this is a physically taxing drill, short distances of 15-30 yards are run.

Focus on correct posture and maximal effort at all times. Maintain an upright body alignment while sprinting; do not bend at the waist. Concentrate on driving the knees high for maximal hip flexion and fully extending the hips to increase stride length. Maintain efficient arm action by keeping the elbows bent at 90 degrees at all times and driving them straight forward and back.

SPRINT WITH PARTNER ASSISTANCE This drill builds on the previous drill, and is slightly more advanced. Two people are paired up in this drill, both wearing belts with the sprint resistor attached. Begin with one partner lined up in front of the other. The partner in front starts to run as fast as possible; when this partner has gone about 5 yards the other partner starts to follow, sprinting as fast as possible. The tubing will be towing the second person forward, causing them to run faster than normal, increasing leg turnover rate. Sprint for a total distance of 20-25 yards and then switch positions. It is important to keep constant tension on the tubes but not overstretch them. This drill provides variety to over speed training. The athlete being towed should focus on quickly moving their legs to maximize the over speed effect of the drill.

LATERAL SHUFFLE WITH PARTNER RESISTANCE Two people with comparable speed are paired up for this drill. One wears the belt with the sprint resistor tubing attached, the other holds the loose end tightly. The tubing should be taut, with little slack. It is important to keep constant tension on the tubes but not overstretch them. Begin with one partner standing beside the other. The partner wearing the tubing starts to side shuffle, keeping their feet under their hips so that their feet do not come together, hips are low, head is up and chest is out. When the first person has gone about 5 yards the other partner starts to jog towards them at a slightly slower pace so that the tubing continues to stretch and the resistance increases. As this is a physically taxing drill, short distances of 15-30 yards are run. Focus on correct posture and maximal effort at all times.

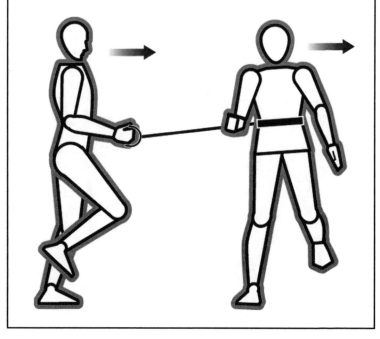

LATERAL SHUFFLE WITH PARTNER ASSISTANCE Two people with comparable speed are paired up for this drill. One wears the belt with the sprint resistor tubing attached, the other holds the loose end tightly. The tubing should be taut, with little slack. It is important to keep constant tension on the tubes but not overstretch them. Begin with one partner standing beside the other. The partner not wearing the tubing walks 5 yards away, stretching the tube. The person wearing the tubing starts to side shuffle towards their partner, keeping their feet under their hips so that their feet do not come together, hips are low, head is up and chest is out. The partner holding the tubing will begin to backpedal, keeping the tension on the tubing. As this is a physically taxing drill, short distances of 15-30 yards are run. Focus on correct posture and maximal effort at all times.

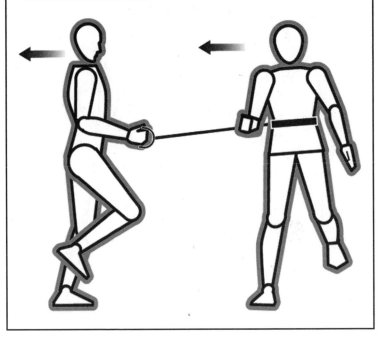

BACKPEDAL WITH PARTNER RESISTANCE Two people with comparable speed are paired up for this drill. One wears the belt with the sprint resistor tubing attached, the other holds the loose end tightly. The tubing should be taut, with little slack. It is important to keep constant tension on the tubes but not overstretch them. Begin with one partner lined up in front of the other. The partner in front starts to backpedal, when they have gone about five yards the other partner starts to follow, jogging at a slightly slower pace so that the tubing continues to stretch and the resistance increases. As this is a physically taxing drill, short distances of 15-30 yards are run. Focus on correct posture and maximal effort at all times. Keep your hips low and shoulders over your feet, head up. Concentrate on moving your legs quickly and staying low. Maintain efficient arm action by keeping the elbows bent at 90 degrees at all times and driving them straight forward and back.

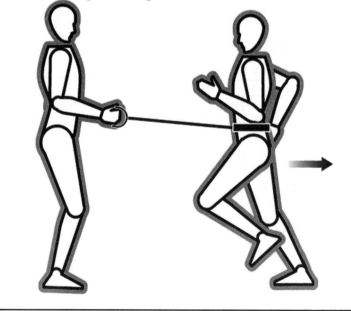

BACKPEDAL WITH PARTNER ASSISTANCE This drill builds on the previous drill, and is slightly more advanced. Two people are paired up in this drill, both wearing belts with the sprint resistor attached. Begin with one partner lined up in front of the other. The partner in front starts to backpedal as fast as possible, when they have gone about five yards the other partner starts to follow, backpedaling as fast as possible. The tubing will be towing the second person backwards, causing them to run faster than normal, increasing leg turnover rate. Sprint for a total distance of 20-25 yards and then switch positions. It is important to keep constant tension on the tubes but not overstretch them. The athlete being towed should focus on quickly moving their legs to maximize the over speed effect of the drill. It is essential that good backpedal technique is used. If the lead partner waits too long to tell the second person to go they will be pulled over backwards and risk hurting themselves.

RESISTED VERTICAL JUMPS Two people are paired for this drill, one is wearing a belt with the sprint resistor attached to the back, and the other stands on the tubing to provide resistance. Stand with feet about shoulder width apart. Swing the arms back and quickly dip until the knees bend to about 120°. Explode upward, extending the knees, hips, ankles and trunk while swinging the arms forward and upward as explosively as possible. Focus on completely extending the body, reaching as high as possible. The arm drive is critical for achieving maximum jump height. The resistor must be taught at the beginning so that resistance is on the tube when the jumper is at the bottom of their dip before exploding upwards.

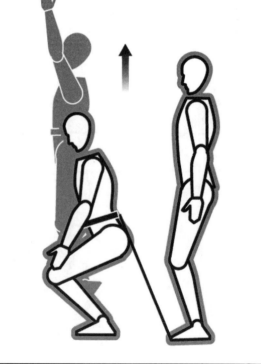

RESISTED LONG JUMP JUMPS Two people are paired for this drill, one is wearing a belt with the sprint resistor attached to the back, and the other stands on the tubing to provide resistance. Stand with feet about shoulder width apart. Swing the arms back and quickly dip until the knees bend to about 120°. Explode forward, extending the knees, hips, ankles and trunk while swinging the arms forward as explosively as possible. Focus on completely extending the body, reaching outward as far as possible, swing your legs under you so that your heels hit the ground first when landing. The arm drive is critical for achieving maximum jump distance. The resistor must be taught at the beginning so that resistance is on the tube when the jumper is at the bottom of their dip before exploding forwards.

EXPLOSIVE LUNGES This is an excellent exercise for those involved in racquet sports or who need to work on first step quickness. Fasten your tubing to a waist high anchor and attach the other end to a belt so that it is stretched directly behind you. Start in an athletic ready position with knees bent, trunk upright and feet just less than shoulder width apart. Explode forward into a lunge, landing with the front leg bent to 90 degrees and the back leg straight. Keeping your trunk upright, drive off the front leg and return to he starting position.

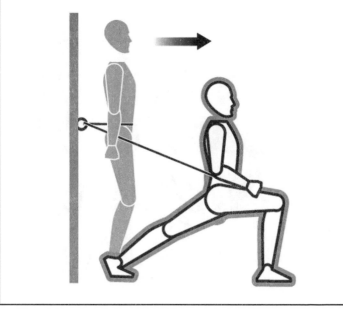

SEE SAWS See saws help develop your ability to perform triple extension movements. Triple extension occurs when the ankle, knee, and hip joints are all extended during a movement. Sports skills like jumping and accelerating out of the athletic ready position to move to a ball or react to an opponent all require triple extension. Facing each other partners will each hold one end of a double tube in both hands at waist height. When both are ready one partner will squat down lowering the tubing handle to shin height at the same time the other partner will extend up onto their toes raising the tubing handle overhead, stretching their body as high as possible. Immediately switch positions so that the partner that was squatting explosively rises up onto their toes, raising the tubing overhead while the other partner squats down.

The movement should start to look like a see saw. Initially you may need to start moving slowly to establish a rhythm but the goal is to do the exercise as quickly as possible.

STANDING BENCH PRESS This movement is useful for athletes who have physical contact with opponents, fighting for position or moving an opponent. Attach the tubing to a chest high hook or other anchor. Face away from the anchor point and grasp a tubing handle in each hand. Stand with feet shoulder width apart one foot slightly ahead of the other. Explosively press your arms forward, extending them fully in front of you.

TUBING JAMMERS Tubing Jammers are the next progression from standing bench presses. Attach the tubing to a chest high hook or other anchor. Face away from the anchor point and grasp a tubing handle in each hand. Stand with feet shoulder width apart in an athletic ready position, knees slightly bent, head up, shoulders back and chest out. Starting with your hands at your chest explode upwards and outwards performing a triple extension, extending your knees, ankles and hips. As you near the top of the triple extension drive your arms forward as quickly as possible. Return to the starting position and repeat as required.

HIP FLEXOR STEP UP The hip flexors are used to raise the knee and are very important muscles for driving the leg forward during sprinting and jumping. The box or bench used for this exercise needs to be high enough to create a 120-degree angle at the knee when the foot is placed on the box. Stand upright with the rubber tubing wrapped around the ankle of one foot and have a partner hold the other end or anchor it at floor height; feet are shoulder width apart, head is up, your chest is out and shoulders are back. Stand 12-18 inches behind the box or bench. Place the entire foot of the leg without the tubing on the top of the box, shifting your weight to the leg on the box. Powerfully extend the knee, hip, and ankle of the foot on the box, and bring your body to a standing position on top of the box. As you reach a full standing position bring the other knee up as high as possible, stretching the tubing. Step off the box, keeping all your weight on your box leg and lightly touch the ground with the non-box leg; do not put any weight on the non-box leg, it is only being used as a guide to tell you when you have gone low enough. Immediately stand back up and drive the knee up again. Keep your trunk upright throughout the movement; avoid bending over from the waist.

CHAPTER 10

Designing Your Program

N ow that you have a repertoire of exercises to choose from you need to start putting them into programs that will meet your training goals. While many people make changes to their programs simply by changing the exercises, there are other factors such as sets and reps, rest and recovery and the speed of exercise that have an impact on your program. Learning to manipulate these variables will give you better results in less time and allow you to create an unlimited number of programs.

Sets and Reps

More than any other factor the combination of sets and reps determines the outcome of the training program. The number of reps determines the resistance that will be used, the lower the reps the greater the resistance. Generally, training with greater resistance for fewer reps builds strength, an intermediate resistance for a moderate number of reps will build muscle size and shape, and a light resistance for many reps will build muscular endurance. The table below summarizes the combination of sets and reps for various training outcomes.

SETS AND REPS

GOAL	MUSCLE SIZE AND SHAPE	STRENGTH	MAXIMUM STRENGTH	MUSCULAR ENDURANCE
Sets per exercise	3-5	3-5	3-4	1-3
Repetitions	8-12	3-6	1-3	25-200
Sets per workout	12-30	10-32	5-20	8-10

Selecting a Resistance to Use

While the rep range gives you a guideline for the amount of resistance to use it is up to you to pick the appropriate resistance for your goal and fitness level. One of the most basic principals of training is the Overload Principle, which states that you need to continually be increasing the physical stress on your body in order for it to continue to adapt and bring you closer to your goals. Choose a resistance that will allow you to just complete the number of reps required for the low end of the rep range for your goal from the table above; use this resistance until you are able to perform the high end of the rep range for all sets, then increase the resistance and start over at the low end of the rep range again.

Total number of sets

It is not necessary to spend hours in the gym to get a good workout and achieve your goals. Many people try to do too much, believing that if one exercise is good more must be better. This is untrue. The stimulus for increases in muscle strength or size is like the button on an elevator: press it and the elevator is coming; pressing the button more often does not get the elevator to your floor any faster. Doing more and more exercises and sets only increases the amount of time needed for recovery between training sessions, it does not provide a greater stimulus.

Initially one to two exercises per body part for a total of 12-24 sets will be adequate, giving you a workout that should last no more than 40 minutes. As your fitness and recovery ability improves you can increase the number of sets up to 30-32 sets per workout, giving you a workout that will take 90-120 minutes.

Rest between sets takes up the majority of the time in a workout. If you find that you cannot get a full workout done in the time you have available, you may want to consider either a split routine or circuit training.

Split Routines

Split routines break the body up so that you are only working a couple of body parts per training session. This will decrease the time needed for each training session but increases the number of times per week that you must work out. Typical groupings for a split routine are chest and triceps; back and biceps; legs and shoulders, with abs done every second workout. Another popular way of dividing things up is to simply split the body into upper and lower halves, working the upper body one day and the lower body the next, followed by a day off before starting the sequence again. Sample workouts in the next chapter for individual body parts will allow you to put together your own split routine program.

Circuit training

Circuit training offers an alternative to the traditional set/rest style of training. Circuit training involves moving from one exercise to another, alternating upper and lower body movements, without any rest between exercises. After you have completed one set of the circuit, typically four to eight exercises, you will take a break. The full body circuit in the next chapter can be done in less than 30 minutes if the gym is not busy.

Rest

Rest refers to the time that is taken between each set of an exercise. The rest between sets allows your body the time to replenish the energy used during the set and plays a role in determining the training effect. The amount of rest that is taken depends upon the duration of work in the strength training session and your training objectives.

Strength

Rest periods for developing strength and maximal strength are quite long, usually three to ten minutes. Strength training with heavy resistance and low reps uses predominantly the anaerobic alactic energy system. The alactic energy system relies on the energy stored in the muscles. Energy is stored in the form of ATP and CP. These two compounds, known as the phosphagens, are available for immediate use. The stored supply of these compounds is relatively small; they can provide energy for about 10-15 seconds of all out strength training effort. Once all the stored energy is used up the body requires about three minutes to fully replace the phosphagens. If the next set is started before the phosphagens are fully restored the muscles will be forced to use the anaerobic lactic energy system. This will result in a build up of lactic acid.

Lactic acid is responsible for the burning sensation in the muscles. It also causes feelings of heaviness and fatigue. A build up of lactic acid will inhibit the quantity and quality of work performed, resulting in fewer strength gains.

Muscle Size and Shape

It is quite common for bodybuilders to take short rest periods between sets, particularly during pre-contest preparation. This is done for a variety of reasons; depletion of carbohydrate stores, to keep metabolism high and burn more calories, and to stimulate muscle growth.

As we already discussed, short rest periods will result in an accumulation of lactic acid. There is some evidence that strength training sessions that result in high lactic acid levels also cause the body to release more growth hormone, one of the hormones responsible for increasing muscle size. Rest periods in bodybuilding programs are typically 30 seconds to two minutes in duration.

Sports Performance

The rest periods between sets for athletes vary depending on the time of the year. They will initially be quite long, three to five minutes during the off season and preseason when strength and power are the main training goals. During the season the rest period should simulate the rest periods that they have in their competitions. For instance if you are a competitive weightlifter and have several minutes between lifts you should take several minutes between your sets. If you are a tennis player and have 20 seconds between points you should limit the rest time between your sets to about 20 seconds. A wrestler who is constantly working for a whole match may use circuit training in season so that they can continuously move from exercise to exercise. Adjusting the rest period between sets to your sport will help you develop the appropriate energy systems and recovery ability between bouts of work.

REST PERIODS BETWEEN SETS

WORK TYPE	REST BETWEEN SETS	REST BETWEEN EXERCISES
Strength	2–3 minutes	2–3 minutes
Maximum Strength	3–5 minutes	5–10 minutes
Muscle Size and Shape	30 seconds– 2 minutes	None
Sports Training	0–several minutes	0–several minutes

Recovery

Recovery, the time between training sessions, depend on your training goals and the number of sets and reps in a workout.

STRESS AND TRAINING ADAPTATIONS

The purpose of training is to create a stress and subsequent adaptation which results in an improved performance. Hans Selye was the first to popularize the concept of adaptations to stress in his book *The Stress of Life*. In this work Selye proposes a three part response to stress called the General Adaptation Syndrome (GAS). The first stage, the alarm stage, is characterized by increases in stress hormones and activation of body defenses. The second stage, the stage of resistance, is a period where your body attempts to adapt so that homeostasis is restored. The third stage, the stage of exhaustion, occurs if the amount of stress is too great for your body to adapt. There is an increase in stress hormones and a reactivation of body defenses as in the alarm stage.

A training session imposes a stress on the body. Following the session there is a decrease in performance as a result of decreased energy stores and or structural damage. At some point in time the body will replenish energy stores and repair damage. If enough time is left before the next training session, a training adaptation can occur and performance will be improved. If inadequate time is left and a training session is started before some level of adaptation occurs, your performance will continue to decrease.

The ideal time to start the next training session is when you reach the peak adaptation part of the curve; this is when your body has gotten as much as it can from the training session. The table below provides some guidelines for recovery periods based on training goals. The recovery number represents the minimum amount of time you should wait between training sessions while the adaptation time is the point where your body is reaching peak adaptation from the previous training session. Note that this table refers to the time needed between training sessions for the same body parts. For instance, if you are following a split routine and are training to increase strength, you may be able to work out every day but would only work each muscle group once every 96 hours.

GOALS	RECOVERY TIME	ADAPTATION TIME
Muscle size and shape	48 hours	72 hours
Strength	48 hours	96 hours
Maximum Strength	72 hours	120 hours
Muscular endurance	24 hours	72 hours

Exercise Speed

Strength increases are specific to the speed of movement at which they are performed. In other words, if you train using slow movements you will increase your strength at low speeds and if you train at high speeds you will get strong at high speeds. This makes speed of movement an important training variable that needs to be considered when designing a strength-training program. In real life you will encounter a variety of speeds of movement, from the slow controlled movements you use when carrying something breakable, to the violent high-speed movements you would use chopping wood or starting a lawn mower. Your strength- training program should reflect this by using a variety of speeds. Start with slow controlled movements for the first few weeks of your program, and gradually increase the speed of movement as the weeks go on until you are performing the exercises in an explosive, dynamic fashion. Keep in mind that moving fast is not a license to cheat or use bad exercise technique. High speed movements must be done with perfect technique if you are to benefit from the exercise.

In the sample workouts in the next chapter the speed of movement is listed using three numbers; 111, 212, etc. These numbers are the three components of a lift; the concentric phase where the weight is lifted, a pause at the top or bottom of the movement and the eccentric phase, where the weight is lowered. An exercise that is listed as a 111 will take you three seconds to complete each rep, and would be considered a moderate speed exercise. In some cases you will see Hold or Explosive.

Hold is used for exercises that have little or no movement, requiring you to hold the position for a period of time rather than perform a number of reps. Explosive is used with the power exercises and indicates that the concentric portion of the exercise is to be done as fast as possible.

Order of Exercises

Placing your exercises in the proper sequence will ensure that you are getting the most benefit out of your workout. One of the goals of exercise sequencing is to arrange the exercises in an order that minimizes the impact of fatigue from exercise to exercise, allowing you to complete the workout before running out of energy. There are several ways of ordering your exercises depending on the equipment and time you have available and your training goals.

DESCENDING ENERGY COST ORDERING

Some ordering plans call for the sequencing of exercises from those that use the most energy to those that use the least. This allows you to train the hardest exercises without fatigue. Some examples of these schemes are as follows:

LARGE MUSCLES TO SMALL MUSCLES

Under this method the largest muscles of the body are trained before the smaller muscles. Training large muscles will require more energy and create more fatigue than training small muscles. The typical order would be:

Thighs and Butt	Abs
Hamstrings	Triceps
Chest	Biceps
Back	Calves
Shoulders	Forearms

MULTI-JOINT TO SINGLE JOINT

Multi-joint exercises are those where more than one major joint in the body is involved in the exercise. For instance, in a deadlift movement occurs at both the hip and knee joints. Movements involving multiple joints require heavier resistances and more energy than single joint movements. Examples of multiple joint movements include:

Squats	Deadlift
Front squats	Overhead press movements
Bench Press	Bent rows
Incline press	Seated rows
Decline Press	

HIGH POWER TO LOW POWER

Power is developed when the resistance you are using is moved at high speed. This increases the energy demand of the activity. If speed of movement decreases, so does power production and the power training effect. The ability to maintain power depends on the body's stores of ATP, which are depleted very quickly. Power training is done early in the training session to take advantage of higher energy levels. The Olympic style weightlifting movements like the power clean, power snatch, push press, and jerk are the most common power movements.

ALTERNATING MUSCLE GROUPS

Alternating muscle groups is another way of preventing fatigue. The objective of this method is to alternate muscles from exercise to exercise. This is usually accomplished by alternating push and pull movements or upper body and lower body movements. For instance if you did an incline press as your first exercise you would want to do a seated row or pull-down as the next exercise because they use unrelated muscle groups. Alternating push-pull exercises is used if you are only training a couple of muscle groups in each session; if you are doing a full body workout alternating upper and lower body is more effective. An example of ordering by alternating muscle groups is:

Push/Pull	**Upper Body/Lower Body**
Incline Bench Press	Bench press
Seated row	Front Squat
Dumbbell Overhead press	Pulldown
Barbell Curl	Seated Leg curls
Triceps Kickbacks	Side lateral raise
	Standing Calf raise
	Alternate Dumbbell curls
	Sit ups
	Triceps pushdowns

PRIORITY ORDERING

Priority ordering refers to sequencing the exercises by order of importance for your training goals. If you were training for rock climbing and need to increase the strength in your hands and fingers you might choose to do forearm and gripping work first in a training session when you are fresh and have the most energy. This approach makes the most sense for activities that rely primarily on small muscle groups that typically fatigue quickly.

WARM UP

Warm up is an essential part of a workout. While originally thought to be primarily a means of preventing injury, it is now commonly accepted that the main purpose of warm up is to improve performance with injury prevention taking a secondary role. The positive effects of warm up occur because muscle temperature is increased, allowing the muscles to contract faster and more forcefully, use oxygen more efficiently, and eliminate waste better.

Types of warm ups

There are three types of warm ups: passive, general and specific. Each has its advantages and disadvantages.

PASSIVE WARM UP

A passive warm up increases temperature through external means. Massage, hot showers, lotions, and heating pads are common forms. Although these methods increase body temperature, they produce little positive effect on performance. A passive warm up, because of increased muscle temperature, may be suitable prior to a stretching exercise but should not be recommended as the sole means of warming up for intense physical activity.

GENERAL WARM UP

A general warm up increases temperature by using movements for the major muscle groups; calisthenics and light jogging activities are most common. This type of warm up is meant to increase temperature in a variety of muscles using general movement patterns. This is a good warm up for a fitness class but should not serve as the sole form of warm up for athletic training or events.

SPECIFIC WARM UP

The specific warm up is designed to prepare you for the specific demands of the upcoming activity. The specific warm up helps psychological readiness, co-ordination of specific movement patterns, and prepares the central nervous system as well as the muscles. A specific warm up usually consists of a simulation of some technical component of the activity at work rates that increase progressively. For example, an Olympic weightlifter will perform the snatch with heavier weights progressively until reaching 80-90% of the opening attempt. Because of the rehearsal component of this type of warm up, it is the preferred method for high speed, strength and power activities.

Designing a warm up

A good warm up has both a general and specific component and may include a passive component if you feel you perform better when you use some sort of a topical analgesic like Tiger Balm.

General Warm Up
FULL BODY CALISTHENICS

A warm up starts with some full body calisthenics. Exercises like jumping jacks, rope jumping, push ups, sit ups, and lunges are full body exercises that will increase body temperature. These exercises should be done for only 3- 5 minutes at a time as the goal of warm up is to increase temperature not create fatigue.

STRETCHING

Dynamic stretching is a more effective means of warm-up stretching than static stretching, meaning that rather than holding a stretch for a period of time, you move through a full range of motion and then back to your starting position immediately without holding the stretch. This is particularly true when you are doing power training. Several studies have shown that a static stretch immediately before power training can significantly decrease subsequent power development.

DURATION OF GENERAL WARM UP

The amount of time needed to warm up depends on the type and intensity of the activity as well as environmental conditions. For someone engaged in a fitness workout program, ten minutes may be sufficient for a warm up. Elite level athletes may require 30 or 40 minutes to warm up depending on the nature of their event, with higher intensity events requiring longer warm ups. Exercising in a warm environment requires a shorter warm up than exercising in a cold one. In a normal environment the onset of sweating is usually a good indicator that body temperature has increased sufficiently.

Specific Warm Up

The nature of the specific warm up depends on the activity to follow. Keep in mind that warm up is just that—warm up, not training. Fatigue should be kept to a minimum during warm up or else the training session will suffer. When resistance training, do at least two sets, one at 50% and one at

75% of the resistance you will be using during the workout, before using the working resistance. Very strong people need to do more sets. Many elite powerlifters and weightlifters use six to eight warm up sets prior to opening attempts in competition. Repetitions in warm up sets are low, 1-4, and done at a controlled speed. Warm up sets are done for every exercise in the program, not just the first exercise.

This chapter has provided you with a framework and background information to help you design your own training programs. The following chapter provides a number of sample workouts that will help clarify these points. The workouts can be used as they are or modified for your situation. If you do decide to create your own program, take your time and use a training log book to record the results of your efforts, which will help you refine your program-designing abilities.

Monitoring Your Progress

Training without monitoring your progress is like driving with your eyes closed—you will get somewhere but you can't be sure where or what shape you'll be in when you arrive. Through daily monitoring you will be able to make the fine adjustments to your program that allow you to continue to progress and recover at the fastest rate possible.

CHARTING YOUR WORKOUTS

A training logbook is the best investment you can make in your athletic career. When used properly it tells you the effectiveness of your training program, your state of recovery, and how well you tolerate training volume or intensity. It also allows you to adjust the program as you go, ensuring optimum progress and performance. Many people use a logbook to record whether they have completed all the activities in a training session. It is also very common for people to record the number of sets, reps, and resistance used in a strength training session.

If you are training to alter you appearance by either gaining muscle mass or losing weight you may want to record your measurements once a month. Standardize the procedures you use for taking measurements: always measure at exactly the same point, wear the same clothing, use a metal tape measure (cloth or plastic tapes can stretch), and measure at the same time of day. This will make your comparisons from month to month more accurate.

Monitoring Recovery

Although many people dislike math or the thought of math, numbers are your friends when it comes to improving your fitness. Recording sets, reps, speed, bodyweight, and time provides a basis for measuring and monitoring training sessions and the program as a whole. The numbers are not the whole story. They will tell you what is happening in a training session but don't help explain why—you need to combine training data with recovery data that measures sleep, soreness and other physiological parameters that will show whether or not you are heading towards overtraining.

Over the years many physiological tests have been developed to try to measure recovery and guide training programs. Blood urea, creatine kinase, hormone levels and ratios, and blood amino acid profiles are just some of the tests that have been used. If you are an elite professional making millions of dollars per year and have access to top medical and physiology labs and consultants, these tests are probably worth using. For everyone else there is a much simpler way that has been shown to be as effective as all the expensive blood work: the recovery questionnaire.

THE RECOVERY QUESTIONNAIRE

The recovery questionnaire is filled out every day of the week whether there is a workout scheduled or not, because you want to be able to measure the effect of a day off as well as a training day. A 2-3 week baseline should be established in the off-season when you are doing little or no training. The baseline is used to measure how far from a fully recovered state you are moving as a result of training and will be referred back to every week, so keep the baseline numbers handy.

Each of the items in the questionnaire is rated on a scale of 1-10, using half points as well as whole numbers. Low numbers are better ratings, for example a rating of 1 on quality of sleep means you had a great night's sleep, a 10 might mean you were up most of the night. The ratings are based on how you felt when you first woke up and got out of bed in the morning. Be honest with yourself, as you will use this information to adjust your program. Body weight should be measured after voiding and before breakfast so that conditions for the weigh-in are standardized. Morning heart rate is measured as soon as you wake up. Keep a watch by your bedside and take a 30 second heart rate count and multiply it by two to get the number of beats per minute.

RECOVERY QUESTIONNAIRE

ITEM	MON	TUES	WED	THURS	FRI	SAT	SUN	AVERAGE	BASELINE
Hours of Sleep									
Sleep Quality									
Muscle Soreness									
Joint Soreness									
General Fatigue									
Desire to Train									
Motivation									
Morning HR									
Bodyweight									

USING THE DATA TO ADJUST THE PROGRAM

All data is compared back to the baseline established at the start of the program. No single variable can assess recovery; the power of the questionnaire comes from the use of multiple variables simultaneously. If you see an increase of two points on the unshaded variables, compared to the baseline, on three or more variables two days in a row, you need to take a day off or cut both the volume and intensity of the day's training in half. If the week average of three of the unshaded items increases by three or more points you need to schedule a recovery week, even if one is not planned in the program.

Morning heart rate and body weight are not included in the daily and weekly analysis because changes in these items are much more gradual than the other factors that are being monitored. Increases in morning heart rate of more than 10 beats per minute for a week or more should be looked at closely, if it is occurring without changes in any of the other variables it may signal a loss of aerobic fitness which may or may not affect your performance, depending on the endurance demands of your sport. If the weekly average is increasing and morning heart rate is high, you need to consider planning a recovery week.

Unintentional decreases in bodyweight are one of the early signs of overtraining. Body weight can fluctuate daily because of hydration levels and what you ate and drank the previous day. Very large people can see their weight change by several pounds from day to day; because of this it is better to use weekly percent changes in body weight to assess your long-term weight profile. If you see a weekly-unintended weight loss of more than two percent something needs to be adjusted in training or diet. First increase fluid intake to see if you are dehydrated because of the week's training schedule and insufficient fluid intake. If the weekly average of other variables is increasing and bodyweight is decreasing, there is a good chance that you are beginning to overtrain and need to schedule a recovery week.

ADDING IN OBSERVATIONS

Outside factors influence your ability to train. You need space to record training observations in your logbook. Observations help explain why you are feeling as you are and why training is going as it is. Record any difficulties that you are having in training or unusual events that may be having an impact on your program. For instance if you had a busy day of classes and skipped lunch, this fact should be recorded in your logbook as it may have an effect on an after-school training session, and if it occurs regularly will help you change the workout to one that you can handle on days you miss lunch. Things to keep track of include but are not limited to; activity outside of training like PE classes, biking or walking to workouts, pick up games with friends, and physical jobs; eating schedules and amounts; work assignments, exams, family commitments and other events that disrupt your normal schedule and increase the stress in your life. As you evaluate changes in your recovery questionnaire these observations will help you determine if an outside cause or the training program is impairing your recovery and progress, and allow you to make adjustments in the appropriate areas of your life.

CHAPTER 11

Sample Workouts

Chest Workout

Individual body part programs are done as part of a split routine, which has been discussed previously. The repetitions listed in the program are for a mixed program that will improve strength and cause a small amount of muscle mass increase, ideal for those seeking a "toned" physique. If you wish to focus primarily on strength, decrease the reps into the 3-5 reps range. If you wish to maximize muscle mass increase the reps into the 10-12 range and add a fourth set to each exercise. Rest periods between sets will be quite long, 2-4 minutes.

EXERCISE	SETS	REPS	SPEED
Bench Press	3	6-8	111
Resisted Push Up	3	6-8	111
Incline Bench Press	3	6-8	111
One Arm Flys	3	6-8	111

Upper Arm Workout

To fully train the upper arms you will need to work both the biceps and triceps. Alternating bicep and tricep exercises distributes the fatigue throughout the upper arm more effectively, allowing you to use a higher resistance tube. The repetitions listed in the program are for a mixed program that will improve strength and cause a small amount of muscle mass increase, ideal for those seeking a "toned" physique. If you wish to focus primarily on strength decrease the reps into the 3-5 reps range. If you wish to maximize muscle mass increase the reps into the 10-12 range and add a fourth set to each exercise. Rest periods between sets will be quite long, 2-4 minutes.

EXERCISE	SETS	REPS	SPEED
Alternate Arm Curls	3	6-8	111
Triceps Pushdown	3	6-8	111
Concentration Curls	3	6-8	111
Lying Triceps Extension	3	6-8	111
Overhead Arm Curls	3	6-8	111
Overhead Triceps Extension	3	6-8	111

Rotator Cuff Workout 1

The rotator cuff stabilizes the shoulder for throwing and arm swing movements. Many people develop rotator cuff injuries because they never train the rotator cuff. One quick test to determine if you need rotator cuff work is to stand facing a mirror with your hands relaxed at your sides. Look in the mirror—if you can see the backs of your hands, you have a muscle imbalance between the muscles on the front of your body that pull your shoulders forwards, and the rotator cuff muscles that keep your shoulders back. If you do have an imbalance do this workout two or three times per week for four weeks and then decrease to one to two times per week.

EXERCISE	SETS	REPS	SPEED
45° raise	3	10-12	212
Internal Rotation	3	10-12	212
Rear Raise	3	10-12	212
External Rotation	3	10-12	212

Rotator Cuff Workout 2

This is a more advanced rotator cuff workout for those who are involved in throwing and ball-striking sports. It can be done twice a week, normally on the same day you would do other shoulder exercises.

EXERCISE	SETS	REPS	SPEED
90-90 External Rotation	3	10-12	111
Overhead Internal Rotation	3	10-12	111
Overhead External Rotation	3	10-12	111
External Rotation	3	10-12	111
Tumbs down low trap exercise	3	10-12	111

Shoulder Workout

A shoulder workout can be combined with a rotator cuff workout or done separately. If you do them separately be careful not to do them on consecutive days; the rotator cuff muscles are involved in other shoulder exercises and making them work every day could lead to injury and overtraining. If you decide to do shoulders and rotator cuff in the same workout, do the shoulder exercises first so that the rotator cuff muscles are not fatigued when they are called upon to stabilize the shoulders. The repetitions listed in the program are for a mixed program that will improve strength and cause a small amount of muscle mass increase, ideal for those seeking a "toned" physique. If you wish to focus primarily on strength decrease the reps into the 3-5 reps range. If you wish to maximize muscle mass increase the reps into the 10-12 range and add a fourth set to each exercise. Rest periods between sets will be quite long, 2-4 minutes.

EXERCISE	SETS	REPS	SPEED
Upright Row	3	6-8	111
Alternating Overhead Press	3	6-8	111
Bent Lateral Raise	3	6-8	111
Side Lateral Raise	3	6-8	111

Upper Back Program

Individual body part programs are done as part of a split routine, which has been discussed previously. The repetitions listed in the program are for a mixed program that will improve strength and cause a small amount of muscle mass increase, ideal for those seeking a "toned" physique. If you wish to focus primarily on strength decrease the reps into the 3-5 reps range. If you wish to maximize muscle mass increase the reps into the 10-12 range and add a fourth set to each exercise. Rest periods between sets will be quite long, 2-4 minutes.

EXERCISE	SETS	REPS	SPEED
Pulldowns	3	6-8	112
Straight arm Pulldown	3	6-8	112
Seated row	3	6-8	112
Low trap exercise	3	6-8	112

Leg Workout

Leg workouts can be tough to do using rubber tubing; you will need a very strong tube or a set of double tubes. In some cases it will be necessary to order bands from www.jumpstretch.com if you are too strong for regular tubing.

Individual body part programs are done as part of a split routine, which has been discussed previously. The repetitions listed in the program are for a mixed program that will improve strength and cause a small amount of muscle mass increase, ideal for those seeking a "toned" physique. If you wish to focus primarily on strength decrease the reps into the 3-5 reps range. If you wish to maximize muscle mass increase the reps into the 10-12 range and add a fourth set to each exercise. Rest periods between sets will be quite long, 2-4 minutes.

EXERCISE	SETS	REPS	SPEED
Squats	3	6-8	112
Crossover Step ups	3	6-8	112
Hip Abduction	3	6-8	112
Hip Adduction	3	6-8	112
Single leg lying Leg Curls	3	6-8	112
Seated calf raise	3	6-8	112

Hip and Butt Workout

Many people want to firm their butt and thighs. While there are aesthetic reasons for working these muscles, increasing strength in this area helps you perform daily activities like stair climbing and can help prevent chronic knee, hip and back pain.

Individual body part programs are done as part of a split routine, which has been discussed previously. The repetitions listed in the program are for a mixed program that will improve strength and cause a small amount of muscle mass increase, ideal for those seeking a "toned" physique. If you wish to focus primarily on strength decrease the reps into the 3-5 reps range. If you wish to maximize muscle mass increase the reps into the 10-12 range and add a fourth set to each exercise. Rest periods between sets will be quite long, 2-4 minutes.

EXERCISE	SETS	REPS	SPEED
The Clam	3	6-8	112
O-Tube hip abduction	3	6-8	112
Glute Press	3	6-8	112
Split squat	3	6-8	112
Hip adduction	3	6-8	112
Hip extension	3	6-8	112

Abdominal Workout 1

Tubing can be a great way to train the abs. Many people forget that the abdominal muscles are like any other muscle, responding best when resistance is applied, not more and more repetitions. The program below is a general strengthening program that hits all areas of the abs. It is a great program for beginners or those interested in overall fitness; it should be done two to three times per week.

EXERCISE	SETS	REPS	SPEED
Curl Ups	3	12-15	222
Side Bends	3	12-15	222
Overhead Crunches	3	12-15	222
Leg Tucks	3	12-15	222

Abdominal Workout 2

This is a more advanced abdominal workout with a greater emphasis on rotational movements, which are important for most sports. The lower rep range means you will need to use a higher resistance tube. Some of the movements are done at high speed which helps improve speed and power in the abdominal muscles to aid throwing and ball-striking activities. If you are not involved in that sort of sport you can decrease the speed and use a 111 tempo.

EXERCISE	SETS	REPS	SPEED
Wood Chops	4	8-10	Explosive -11
Twisting overhead crunches	4	8-10	111
Paddlers	4	8-10	Explosive 12
Leg Raises	4	8-10	111
Stability Ball Side Bends	4	8-10	121

Road Warrior Combo Workout

Busy business people often have difficulty finding the time to do a good workout, particularly when they are traveling; most hotels offer a fitness facility but rarely are they staffed and you can never count on the availability or quality of the equipment. Tubing is the ideal training tool for the business traveler—it can easily fit in a suitcase and it can be used anywhere. If you aren't self conscious, you could even get in a few sets while waiting for a flight at the airport.

This workout is a combo workout. Combo exercises are exercises that flow into each other, allowing them to be performed without stopping, substantially decreasing the time to do the workout. Because there is no rest between the exercises in each combo, a combo can become very fatiguing and you may find yourself out of breath. Be sure to listen to your body and not push yourself too hard, particularly if you are doing the workout alone in a hotel room after a day of travel where you may already be fatigued, stressed and partially dehydrated because of air travel.

For each of the combos listed in the program move immediately from one exercise to the next as if they were one exercise, but do not take short cuts to make the exercise easier. The repetitions listed in the program are for a mixed program that will improve strength and cause a small amount of muscle mass increase, ideal for those seeking a "toned" physique. If you wish to focus primarily on strength decrease the reps into the 3-5 reps range. If you wish to maximize muscle mass increase the reps into the 10-12 range and add a fourth set to each exercise. Rest periods between sets will be quite long, 2-4 minutes. The speed recommendation is for each exercise of the combo, not the whole combo.

EXERCISE	SETS	REPS	SPEED
Curl/overhead press/ triceps extension	3	6-8	212
Seated leg press/calf press	3	6-8	212
Pulldown/overhead crunch	3	6-8	212
Upright row/Front raise	3	6-8	212

Upper body Strength Maintenance Program

Some people may wish to use tubing occasionally to supplement a free weight or machine-based program when they cannot get to the gym for their normal workout. This program can be used as a light day between heavy training sessions, or as a maintenance day when traveling so that you do not lose your hard earned fitness gains. It is also a great program for athletes who need to maintain their strength during the competitive season or those who have reached their goals and just want to maintain their present levels of fitness and strength.

EXERCISE	SETS	REPS	SPEED
90-90 External rotation	3	6	212
Incline press	3	6	212
One arm row	3	6	212
Pulldowns	3	6	212
Triceps Pushdowns	3	6	212
Arm curls	3	6	212

Lower body Strength Maintenance Program

Some people may wish to use tubing occasionally to supplement a free weight or machine-based program when they cannot get to the gym for their normal workout. This program can be used as a light day between heavy training sessions or as a maintenance day when traveling so that you do not lose your hard earned fitness gains. It is also a great program for athletes who need to maintain their strength during the competitive season or those who have reached their goals and just want to maintain their present levels of fitness and strength.

EXERCISE	SETS	REPS	SPEED
Squat	3	6	212
Lying leg curl	3	6	212
One arm row	3	6	212
Hip extension	3	6	212
Seated calf press	3	6	212
Hip adduction	3	6	212

20 minute Circuit

This full body circuit can be completed in about 20 minutes if you do not take too long setting up each exercise. Move as quickly as possible from exercise to exercise, taking a rest only after you have completed the whole circuit. When you can do the prescribed number of reps in the prescribed time, increase the resistance you are using.

EXERCISE	Circuit I Time/reps	Circuit II Time/reps	Circuit III Time/reps	Circuit IV Time/reps	Circuit V Time/reps	TOTALS
Seated Row	15s/8	15s/8	15s/8	15s/8	15s/0	32 reps
Leg Press	15s/6	15s/6	15s/6	15s/6	15s/6	30 reps
Bench Press	15s/6	15s/6	15s/6	15s/6	15s/6	30 reps
Leg Curl	15s/6	15s/6	15s/6	15s/6	15s/6	30 reps
Arm Curl	15s/10	15s/10	15s/10	15s/0	15s/0	30 reps
Calf Raise	15s/15	15s/15	15s/0	15s/0	15s/0	30 reps
Overhead Press	15s/6	15s/6	15s/6	15s/6	15s/6	30 reps
Deadlift	15s/6	15s/6	15s/6	15s/6	15s/6	30 reps
Triceps Pushdown	15s/10	15s/10	15s/10	15s/0	15s/0	30 reps
	Rest 2 min	Rest 2 min	Rest 2 min	Rest 2 min		

Sprint Speed Workout

Improving sprint speed requires both assisted and resisted running as well as technical work. This workout combines tubing exercises and normal sprints to help those interested in improving their straight ahead running speed. The descriptions of the non-tubing exercises are not included in this book but they should be quite obvious from their names. If you are stuck on an exercise you can contact us at www.strengthpro.com and we will send you a description.

EXERCISE	SETS	DISTANCE	REST
Sprint starts	4	10 yards	60 s
High Knee sprints	3	10 yards	60s
Butt Kick Sprints	3	10 yards	60s
Sprint with partner resistance	3	20 yards	120s
Sprint with Partner assistance	3	20 yards	120s
Hip Flexor Step Ups	3	6 reps each leg	180s

Sport Speed Workout

Sport speed is different that sprint speed. Where sprint speed focuses on straight ahead running speed, sport speed focuses on developing speed in all directions and the ability to change directions. As with sprint speed, improving sport speed requires technical training as well as physical conditioning. This workout should be part of an overall speed, quickness and agility program that uses a wide variety of drills and exercises in all movement planes and directions.

EXERCISE	SETS	DISTANCE	REST
Sprint with partner assistance	3	15 yards	60 s
Lateral Shuffle with partner assistance	3	15 yards	60s
Backpedal with partner assistance	3	15 yards	60s

Sprint with partner resistance	4	20 yards	120s
Lateral shuffle with partner resistance	4	20 yards	120s
Backpedal with partner resistance	4	20 yards	120s

Full body Workout 1

This program is designed to build strength in all muscles. Over a three week period you will gradually increase the weight you are using and decrease the number of reps. At the end of the three weeks decrease the weight a bit and increase the reps back to the week 1 reps.

EXERCISE	SETS	REPS (one week each box)			SPEED
Squats	4	8	6	4	111
Incline Bench Press	4	8	6	4	111
Pulldowns	4	8	6	4	111
Side Lateral Raise	4	8	6	4	111
Low trap exercise	4	8	6	4	111
Alternate arm curls	4	8	6	4	111
Lying triceps extension	4	8	6	4	111

Full body workout 2

This program is a continuation of Full Body Workout 1 and should be used after two or three cycles of Full Body Workout 1; it is very high intensity and not meant for beginners. This program will peak your strength level. Do only one cycle of this program before switching back to something less intense. Rest periods between sets need to be quite long, three to five minutes, and the program should be done twice a week at most.

EXERCISE	SETS	REPS (one week each box)			SPEED
Deadlift	4	6	4	3	111
Resisted Push up	4	6	4	3	111
Alternate overhead press	4	6	4	3	111
One arm row	4	6	4	3	111
Bent lateral raise	4	6	4	3	111
Arm curls	4	6	4	3	111
Triceps pushdowns	4	6	4	3	111

Unilateral Full body workout

Muscle imbalances between the right and left sides of the body increase the risk of developing chronic injuries. Previous injury, sports that emphasize the use of one side of the body over the other, and handedness are the most common causes of muscle imbalances and all of us suffer from them to one degree or another. Correcting these imbalances is one of the main goals of a strength training program. Training with tubing is a great start to correcting imbalances because the individual handles on the tubing force the right and left sides of the body to work independently. The program below takes working each side of the body to a new level by working one side at a time, allowing you to focus completely on that side of the body and the muscles involved in the movement.

EXERCISE	SETS	REPS	SPEED
Single-leg leg press	3	10-12	212
Standing leg curl	3	10-12	212

One arm flys	3	10-12	212
Alternate seated overhead press	3	10-12	212
Alternate straight arm pulldown	3	10-12	212
Concentration curl	3	10-12	212
Overhead triceps extension	3	10-12	212
Trunk rotations	3	10-12	212

Sport-Specific Programs

In order to be successful at a sport you must train many different physical traits, speed, strength, power, aerobic fitness, anaerobic fitness, agility, flexibility and technique. No single training method will give you all these qualities. Tubing training can help increase strength, speed and power.

TENNIS PROGRAM

The program below is designed to address the muscles and movements most important for tennis players. Use this program two to three times a week in conjunction with skill training and the sport speed program above.

EXERCISE	SETS	REPS (one week each box)			SPEED
Explosive Lunges	4	10	8	6	111
The clam	4	10	8	6	111
90-90 Internal rotation	4	10	8	6	111
90-90 external rotation	4	10	8	6	111
Backhands	4	10	8	6	111
Forehands	4	10	8	6	111
Windups	4	10	8	6	111

BASEBALL PROGRAM

The program below is designed to address the muscles and movements most important for baseball players. Use this program two to three times a week in conjunction with skill training and the sport speed program above.

EXERCISE	SETS	REPS (one week each box)			SPEED
Split squats	4	10	8	6	111
Explosive lunges	4	10	8	6	111
Overhead internal rotation	4	10	8	6	111
Overhead external rotation	4	10	8	6	111
Swings	4	10	8	6	111
Throws	4	10	8	6	111
Windups	4	10	8	6	111

FOOTBALL PROGRAM

The program below is designed to address the muscles and movements most important for football players. Use this program two to three times a week in conjunction with skill training and the sport speed and sprint speed programs above.

EXERCISE	SETS	REPS (one week each box)			SPEED
Squat	4	10	8	6	111
Deadlift	4	10	8	6	111
Standing row	4	10	8	6	111
Standing bench press	4	10	8	6	111

Tubing Jammers	4	10 8 6		111
Hip Flexor Step Up	4	10 8 6		111
Leg raises	4	10 8 6		111

HOCKEY PROGRAMS

The program below is designed to address the muscles and movements most important for hockey players. Use this program two to three times a week in conjunction with skill training and the sport speed and sprint speed programs above.

EXERCISE	SETS	REPS (one week each box)			SPEED
Squat	4	10	8	6	111
Deadlift	4	10	8	6	111
Standing row	4	10	8	6	111
Standing bench press	4	10	8	6	111
Tubing Jammers	4	10	8	6	111
Swings	4	10	8	6	111
Wind ups	4	10	8	6	111

BASKETBALL PROGRAM

The program below is designed to address the muscles and movements most important for basketball players. Use this program two to three times a week in conjunction with skill training and the sport speed and sprint speed programs above.

EXERCISE	SETS	REPS (one week each box)			SPEED
Squat	4	10	8	6	111
Resisted vertical jump	4	10	8	6	111
Explosive lunge	4	10	8	6	111
Standing bench press	4	10	8	6	111
Overhead triceps extension	4	10	8	6	111
Hip Flexor Step Up	4	10	8	6	111
Trunk rotations	4	10	8	6	111

VOLLEYBALL PROGRAM

The program below is designed to address the muscles and movements most important for volleyball players. Use this program two to three times a week in conjunction with skill training and the sport speed and sprint speed programs above.

EXERCISE	SETS	REPS (one week each box)			SPEED
Squat	4	10	8	6	111
Resisted vertical jump	4	10	8	6	111
Explosive lunge	4	10	8	6	111
Overhead press	4	10	8	6	111
Wind ups	4	10	8	6	111
Throws	4	10	8	6	111
Swings	4	10	8	6	111

INDEX